A SELECTION OF
LONDON'S
Most Interesting
PUBS

DAVID GAMMELL

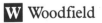 Woodfield

Illustrations by Helen Giaquinto

U.S. Edition first published by:
Sterling/Woodfield
7 Hampton Bays
NY 11946 • USA

ISBN 1 873203 – 16 – 0

Printed and bound in Great Britain by
Biddles Ltd, Guildford and King's Lynn

The Mayflower

Contents

INTRODUCTION

Greater London comprises 570 square miles. To sample every pub therein would be to set out for 'That bourne from which no man returns' yet somewhere in this vast labyrinth of bricks and mortar there is certain to be a pub that will appeal to your own tastes. The question is ... how do you find it?

This book does it for you; not merely by locating it but by describing it's personality before you set out. The pubs included are a personal selection from many thousands. Directions of how to get to each specific pub are given in terms of public transport – mainly London's Underground – which I believe is the easiest system in the world for a stranger to comprehend. Buses are more difficult to understand; the visitor may have the right bus number but be going in the wrong direction because the traffic flow in London is the reverse (mainly) from the rest of the world.

The personality of any chosen pub reflects its customers' tastes; there are Traditional pubs, Historical pubs, Literary pubs, Theatre pubs, Gay pubs, Drag pubs, Boxer's pubs, Actors pubs, ad infinitum. There are pubs that bring back the lively Cockney atmosphere of the Music Hall (Vaudeville) which is a rebirth since it started in pubs. There are pubs which offer theatre from Shakespeare to Kafka, pubs where you may sit down to a five course dinner then sit back to enjoy the show. There are pubs which offer a jazz – there is something about the atmosphere of a pub which makes it ideal for the blast of jazz. Go down to a pub like The Prince of Orange in Cockney Rotherhithe where, in winter, the chill mists may swirl in from the river but – on a jazz night – the atmosphere inside is kin to a red hot Tent Meeting.

Visitors on holiday are apt to eat lunch where the pangs of hunger strike. Should they be in a pub, succour is nigh, ranging from the skilled hands of a chef to the humble but willing hands of 'The Missus' always ready to pop into the kitchen to knock up a sandwich. The visitor has to be briefed about the British sandwich. It is very tasty but compared to, say, the American sandwich, it would appear to be suffering from pernicious anemia... a pale specimen loitering at a tea party on the lawn. The visitor with a hearty appetite is advised to go for the 'Pub Lunch' which most pubs provide.

The hot pub lunch consists of such dishes as Shepherd's pie – a savoury dish of meat and vegetables cooked in the oven and topped with mashed potatoes lightly grilled before serving, grilled sausages are served with crusty bread with pickles on the side, Welsh rarebit (cheese grilled on toast), hot beef sandwiches, meat pies and sometimes an invention of the cook which lends itself to fast food service. There are many pubs – usually denominated as Traditional pubs in the book which serve four or five course lunches where the menu is equal to a good restaurant but not as expensive.

Pubs also serve cold lunches such as a 'Ploughman's Lunch' consisting of a hunk of cheese with crusty bread, butter and peculiarly British pickles served on the side. It may add to your appetite when eating the Ploughman's that you are following in the footsteps of Geoffrey Chaucer when he set out with the other 'Nine and twenty sundry folk' from London's Tabard Inn on their pilgrimage to Canterbury (don't rush to see the Tabard Inn for it is long gone and the pub that bears the name is a nondescript place in a dreary neighbourhood).

Finally, the Government realised that pubs are a part of our traditions too and now goes about slapping preservation orders on historical ones. In the Flask at Highgate the barmaid was heard to complain:

"the blessed floor slopes backwards but the Ministry of Ag & Fish – or whatever – won't allow the 'Guvner' to fix it 'cause it's got a preservation order on it".

Pubs are quite rigidly controlled by the law. A landlord has to have a licence from a magistrate before he can open the doors of his pub, and he must open it promptly at 11.00am and close it at 11.00pm – which is like trying to stop a dog fight by lecturing the animals. The opening on time is no problem – there is always someone desperately kicking at he door ... but to get them out at closing time – with "Time, Gentlemen please!" ignored – is a horse of a different colour. In practice the Landlord keeps on the right side of the law by simply 'putting the towel up': i.e. at 11pm he places a towel over the handles of the beer pumps as an indication that neither love nor money could buy another drink. Youth is protected from itself, too by not being allowed in a pub under the age of eighteen.

Pubs located in 'The City' (The Financial district) where everyone goes home early, are allowed to close by 9pm at the latest. Obviously the time to visit a City pub is at lunchtime when they are vibrant.

Pubs located in markets are a law unto themselves since they are allowed to open at market hours when the sun is hardly over the yardarm – say 6am.

It is the personal atmosphere that makes or breaks a pub. One can tell the moment the door swings open; if the few people in the bar turn their heads to stare, there is nothing inside to interest you. If there is the subdued roar of conversation that goes with people interested in what they are saying, go in.

TRADITIONAL PUBS

JACK STRAW'S CASTLE
North End Way, Hampstead Heath, NW3

How to get there

Underground to Hampstead (Northern line). Walk up Heath Street past the pond to North Way. Jack Straw's Castle is the large white building on the left past the pond.

Magnificently situated on the highest spot in London to give views for miles around, the pub has been, and still is, a well-known landmark to Londoners. Charles Dickens, that most gregarious of Londoners, loved the place and would often walk across the heath to eat a chop and drink a glass of wine in it's restaurant.

With an indulgence in that wry humour for which Londoners are noted, the pub is named after a revolutionary! Jack Straw was a friend and comrade in arms of Watt Tyler, a man of Kent, who in 1381 raised a force of 60,000 men to march on London in protest against Richard II's Poll Tax.

To show earnest intent the Revolutionaries set about wrecking a few things.

Jack Straw was given the task of demolishing the house of Sir Robert Hales – the enforcer of the tax. This accomplished he camped out on the heath at the spot which was to be called after him. His brief but exciting life came to an end shortly after when the revolutionary leader Watt Tyler was stabbed to death by the Lord Mayor of London and his supporters melted away. It is interesting to note that the dagger still appears in the coat of arms of London – appropriately in red.

After the demise of his leader, Jack Straw was apprehended at his castle lair and hanged on an adjacent tree but his name still lives on in this handsome pub.

One of Jack Straw's comrades – a man called John Ball – had a poetical way of expressing things revolutionary; he wrote "When Adam delved and Eve span, who then was the gentleman." His reward for this pertinent phrase was the same as Jack Straw's.

These historical events happened in 1381, but here is a history of at least an ale house on the site a century before.

At Bank Holiday times – Easter and August – a gigantic fair spreads itself over many acres of the heath. Mums and Dads eat jellied eels and the kids break their teeth on sticks of pepper- mint rock in between hurling balls at coconuts or being whirled around by machines cunningly designed to frighten. In the evening they come to Jack Straw's Castle – to the enormous bar on the ground floor where huge plates of such delicacies as steak and kidney pie are available.

If you should prefer the beer garden you may sit outside under a venerable tree confronted by two great casts of unicorns who wear daisy chains around their necks.

Hampstead, residentially, is in the Stockbroker Belt and the local residents are apt to turn up their noses at the Bank Holi- day crowds and go upstairs to the beautiful Turret bar which is surrounded by windows which command a view over London one way and the purlieus of the heath the other way. The pretty young barmaid will tell you, in a soft Galway brogue; "sure on a clear day you can see for twenty mile or more" which is stretching it a bit, but the view is as extensive of London as you will get where "With a ladder and some glasses you can see the Hackney Marshes – if it wasn't for the houses in between".

Indubitably Jack Straw's Castle is a handsome pub. To sit at a table in the restaurant that curves along the facade of the inner courtyard overlooking the people in the beer garden down below, is very pleasant. To quote Dickens "To climb the steep slopes of the Vale of Heath; to watch the kids sailing their boats on the still waters of the Leg of Mutton Pond before strolling on to the refreshments at Jack Straw's is a salubrious experience."

Their has been a building on the site for six centuries but the present building dates from 1872. It was designed by Raymond Erith who rebuilt the Prime Minister's house at N⁰· 10 Downing Street.

THE HOOP & GRAPES
47 Aldgate High Street, EC3

How to get there
Underground (Circle line) to Aldgate station. From the station, cross over Aldgate High Street to number 47.

In 1666, the Great Fires of London raged through the City of London destroying four fifths – including the original St Paul's Cathedral. By some quirk of fate it failed to destroy N⁰· 47 Aldgate High Street which was then occupied by a vintner. Nowadays it is occupied by the Hoop & Grapes.

It still retains its Jacobean staircase and panelling, in fact, the building has been completely restored to its original image. The timber frame and brick interior walls have been ex- posed to the light of day, a stone flagged floor has been in- stalled and a conservatory has been built and lighted by daylight from overhead.

The interior of the Hoop & Grapes.

To recall its days as a vintner's, wine casks – looking huge under the low ceilings – fill up the empty spaces and give it a worked in look. Solid oak tables and benches complete the impres- sion of being in an inn of the 17th century.

To celebrate its reopening after the restoration work, the City of London Ale Conners – an ancient office, redundant but still existent, were invited to perform a ceremony of the middle ages. In those days no ale could be sold before it had been approved by the Ale Connor and a publican who wished to advertise that his ale had been conned would hang out an ale garland to announce the fact that his ale had been approved "Of good price and body and not obnoxious nor likely to be injurious to the health of Tenants, nor hurtful to a man's stomach." After the ceremonious conning had been performed at the Hoop & Grapes "God bless the Queen!" was toasted in a libation of the said beer.

It is not only the age of the Hoop & Grapes that makes it attractive (it claims to be the oldest original pub in London) or its comeliness, but also its homeliness. It is close to Middlesex Street famous for a market known as "Petticoat Lane" which is held there on a Sunday morning. Then the pub is crowded with shoppers from "the lane". It is a salubrious experience to listen to 20th century Cockneys discussing the antics of the pedlars "down The Lane" in the halls of their ancestors and one that is worth foregoing the Sunday morning "lie in" for. There is a lot of food – like hot beef sandwiches – sold on Sunday morning at the Hoop & Grapes, so you may assume it to be fresh.

The pub does not open all day Saturday and closes early on Sunday evening when the crowds from "The Lane" have by then gone home.

The atmosphere of the Hoop & Grapes blends the historic with the homely to give a sense of continuity.

THE SILVER CROSS
34 Whitehall, SW1

How to get there
Underground (Northern, Bakerloo, Jubilee) to Charing Cross. From station walk south to Whitehall. The pub

is on the left hand side of Whitehall just before Great Scotland Yard.

This pub was once a brothel. A long time ago, be warned. King Charles 1st granted it a license. It was obviously a high-class brothel. Even today it has a beautiful ceiling on which there is a preservation order. Presumably, whilst engaged in their professional pursuits the ladies of the house were in an excellent position to enjoy its artistic qualities.

The Silver Cross is remarkable for being one of the four pubs within the "liberty of the palace of St James". The pubs are The Ship, The Shades, The Clarence and the Silver Cross. They are licensed by The Board of Green Cloth which also sets the rules for the conduct of the monarch's London homes. Each year the innkeeper is summoned, in ancient language, to appear before The Board of Green Cloth to prove that his premises are being conducted in an orderly manner as a condition for renewing his licence. It was so different when the monarch alone made the rules.

Today's pub is a pleasant place with comfortable leather armchairs arranged on a cold day around a blazing fire in the open fireplace. It has an excellent lunch counter serving pub lunches at reasonable prices. It is open between 11.00am and 11.00pm for the sale of alcoholic drinks, but it also serves non-alcoholic drinks like tea and coffee before these hours.

It may be said to be in the very heart of Tourist land – the Mounted Horse Guards are within a hundred yards – and the place is a babble of tongues from the four quarters of the world – but considering its history, it is too interesting to pass by. In any case one can rest those aching feet and emulate its long-gone occupants and admire the ceiling.

THE GATEHOUSE
Highgate High Street, N19

How to get there
Underground to Archway (Northern line). From the Underground station either walk up Highgate Hill to the far end of Highgate Village (about one mile) or take a No. 210 bus to Highgate school which is right opposite to the Gatehouse.

The historical significance of Highgate is that it was the gate into London from the North. Many a canny Northerner came down what was always known as the Great North Road to make his fortune in the metropolis – including Dick Wittington who became Lord Mayor of London. The story has it that as a young man; depressed and defeated he was making his way up Highgate Hill on his way back to the North when he heard Bow Bells ring a tune which said to him "Turn again Dick Wittington Lord Mayor of London".

Highgate has a famous cemetery wherein, amongst the remains of other famous people lie those of Karl Marx, who died in one of the boroughs whose boundaries meet in Highgate. The pub has a history that goes back for 500 years. It stands by the High Gate - high enough to allow passage of a horse with a high pack – which gives its name to the area.

The interesting part of its history is that it was the scene of a rustic ceremony that continued for centuries. The ceremony was called "Swearing on the Horns".

The "Swearer In" was dressed in black gown and bands and wore a wig and mask. He was accompanied by his clerk carrying a pair of horns mounted on a stick. The pair inducted the neophyte into the "Order of The Horns by having him recite an oath in which he swore "Never to drink small beer when he could get strong, nor kiss the maid when he could kiss the Mistress". At the end of the ceremony, the gullible novice was sworn in "Upstanding and uncovered" to acknowledge the Landlord as a Father. He thereupon showed his filial devotion by buying wine all round.

It was a harmless rustic rumpus which became so popular that the query "Have you been sworn in on the horns yet"? became a catch word. One can imagine the innuendoes offered to a novice to lead him on. The Gatehouse which stood by the entrance gate from the North of England was in a position to provide a supply of fresh victims as they came in for refreshment. It must have stimulated trade, too.

The present tavern was built in 1763. At one time the County of Middlesex sessions were held here. It happened that the bound- aries of the boroughs of Hornsey and St

Pancras met within the premises of the tavern. Hence when the sessions were held, the parts in Hornsey were roped off from those of St Pancras.

In the year 1409 Henry Smith paid a rent of 30 shillings for the "farming of the toll".

Today the Gatehouse is a shining place where everything that can be polished shines until it glitters. Damask table clothes in its restaurant convey a feeling of luxury that goes with the cooking. It stands in one of the most attractive of "the villages" that surprise the visitor when he enters a rural scene set in the thick of the great Metropolis. It is the sort of place where one takes someone for a treat. It has the usual opening hours of 11.00am to 11.00pm.

THE SPANIARDS
Spaniards Road, Hampstead, NW3

How to get there
Underground (Northern line) to Hampstead. Walk up Heath Street, then along Spaniards Road until you see the traffic jam which is caused by the Toll gate outside The Spaniards Inn. Alternatively take a taxi.

There is an air of romance about this place. Set in a lonely place on the edge of the heath, it has sheltered tragic lovers, ambassadors, poets and writers, rioters and highwaymen. Its very name invokes a legend of two Spanish brothers who owned it. Both loved the same woman. They duelled to the death of one.

The highwayman was Dick Turpin who on occasion stabled his horse Black Bess, there. Both actually existed and are still fondly remembered by Londoners who characteristically favour the hunted rather than the hunter. Even if the cobbled yard is now a car park, Dick Turpin and Black Bess are a legend that still haunts the place.

The Inn is still a genuine 18th century building. Inside the ceilings are supported by oak beams and the walls arc oak pa- nelled; there are cosy nooks furnished with oak settles. In this atmosphere one wants to believe the legends they seem so plausible.

One legend concerns a landlord named Miles Thomas who was the incumbent during the period of the Gordon Riots. Having torched Lord Mansfield's London home the cry went up "To Kenwood!" his beautiful home on Hampstead Heath.

On the way to Kenwood the rioters couldn't resist the good ale at the Spaniards to prime them with "Dutch Courage". Artful Thomas met them at the door with open arms and the injunction "help yourself boys, cellar and all!" But secretly he had already sent a lad to gallop to the barracks of the Horseguards; meanwhile he plied the rioters with his best booze. By the time the troopers arrived the undisciplined mob were stupid with drink and were soon dispersed by the flailing sabres of the troopers.

There is nothing spurious about the hospitality of the inn today it sells Bass and Charrington best ales and wines and spirits. The food is tasteful and imaginatively cooked. At lunch time they have excellent hot and cold fare.

In the summer you can sit in the rose garden and drink where once Byron and Shelley imbibed. It has great literary associations. Keats lived on the other side of the Heath. Like Dickens he would have strolled across to drink the ale and smell the roses.

All the poets, writers, rioters and highwaymen have long gone but the Spaniards goes on doing what it has always done, dispensing hospitality.

THE GEORGE INN
Borough High Street, SE1

How to get there
British Rail to London Bridge or Underground (Northern line) to London Bridge. From station walk down station approach and turn left into Borough High Street. Look for massive gates on left that enclose the courtyard of the inn.

This is the only 17th century coaching inn left in London in its present form. Built in 1677, it is a gracious three storey structure with balustraded balconies overlooking a great courtyard where once stagecoaches arrived and departed.

This is Dickens country. Relics from his life hang on the wall - but he only became a patron of the place after he had become rich and famous. As a child, visiting his father in the Marshalsea prison just down the road, he would have been too poor to enter. In *Little Dorritt* he has Pip go into The George to write begging letters.

Some of the historical inns of the neighbourhood have long since been demolished – notably the Tabard from which Geoffrey Chaucer set out on his pilgrimage to Canterbury and the White Hart where Jack Cade set up his revolutionary headquarters, but the George has been acquired by The National Trust and remains preserved for posterity.

It is not only the outside of the pub that has been preserved. Inside, the low ceilings supported by oak beams and pillars, the panelled walls, the leaded windows are completely in character because they are originals.

When The George was a coaching inn, the Taproom on the ground floor saw the outside passengers (booked in the cheapest seats) huddled together far from the fire, stealing timid glances down the room to where the Drivers spread their legs before a blazing fire; pewter mug in hand, ready to answer questions; not only "How long before we reach Malling", but also "Will there be highwaymen on Black Heath?" The inside passengers would tend to order quarterns of gin rather than beer from the tap.

There is a large clock called The Parliament clock on the wall of the Tap Room. In 1797 when Parliament put a five shilling tax on clocks, the parsimonious elected to rely on public clocks. In the vicinity of The George they would send The Boy round to see the time. The old clock is still there giving accurate time as it did when Dickens, maybe checked his watch, as well as all the Prime Ministers, Field Marshals, Princes and Film Stars who at one time or another, patronized the place since it is known all over the World.

A pamphlet written by Robert Barker, tells an anecdote about Winston Churchill who brought his own wine to lunch. When he received the bill an item "To Corkage; one shilling and six- pence" was included.

The George.

From the same source came the story that owing to the failure of His Majesty's Mint to issue coins there was a shortage of halfpennies and farthings, which decide the incumbent Landlord to issue his own tokens in lieu. On one side he had his own name with St George & the Dragon and on the other in Southwarke in the field."

The George is a great place for fraternities to meet. On Shakespeare's birthday (April 23rd) and on Dicken's birthday (February 7th) plays are performed in celebration.

Some eccentric types are attracted by the historical setting also. The Medieval Combat Society uses the courtyard to stage hand to hand combats as in Medieval times. On these occasions blood flows freely, but Guy's Hospital, which looms over the courtyard, is on hand to give succour to the wounded.

Not only are the inn's gastronomic abilities tested by the famous. The enthusiastic beer drinkers of The Real Ale persuasion have put The George on their list.

Looking down on to the courtyard one can imagine Sam Weller buckling the horses into their harness; imagine the spirited ring of the coachman's horn echoing under the arched exit; the hooves striking sparks from the cobblestones as the horses heave into their collars to set out on the first stage of the long journey to Canterbury or Dover.

THE ANCHOR INN
Bankside, Southwark

How to get there
Underground (Northern line) to London Bridge. Walk down the station approach and cross the road to the south-east corner of London Bridge overlooking the ancient church of St Mary Overie (Now called Southwark Cathedral). John Harvard who founded Harvard University was christened here. His father was a local butcher and St Mary's was the family's parish church.

From your starting point on the bridge look for a flight of steps which will take you down past the Borough Market (oldest in London). Walk down Cathedral Street past St Saviour's Dock into Clink Street.

The Anchor sits on the bank of the river Thames with a perfect view of Wren's masterpiece, St Paul's Cathedral, looming on the other bank. In Shakespeare's time this area was the pleasure ground for the common people. It contained not only The Globe Theatre, where his company, the King's Men, for which he was the playwright, performed his plays, but also the bear pits, the ale houses and the brothels.

The Anchor may have ancient sinews but they beat with life as they did when Shakespeare worked his magic just around the corner. The site of the Globe Theatre is now the Bear Garden Museum.

A modern visitor may saunter round to identify streets called Bear Garden, Skin Market and Clink Street; it is not difficult to guess the nature of the pleasures to be sought in the first two but Clink Street held only pain and remorse since it contained a prison which, incidentally, perpetuated a slang word for prison in the English language. In colloquial English, to go to prison is to go to the 'Clink'. The Clink was the Bishop of Winchester's property. It was destroyed in the 17th century, which was a pity. After all, there are not many private enterprise gaols.

The Anchor was built in 1770, after the original had been destroyed. It was here that Dr. Johnson lived for a year while compiling his English dictionary or lexicon.

The Inn is built within the precincts of the brewery – a peculiar place to nourish culture, but Henry Thrale, the owner, and his wife made it their task to nourish the indigent Johnson so that he could continue to nourish their minds with his conversation. Today's owners, Barclay Perkins, have made a good job of preserving the original atmosphere, although what was once the kitchen, with sanded floor and original fireplace, has been rebuilt and named, somewhat pompously, 'The Thrale Room'. The crooked ceilings supported by smoke-blackened beams are still there.

A tour of the building gives insight into various landlords minds over the years as they added what they considered to be improvements or boarded up what they considered eyesores. One opens a cupboard to discover a concealed staircase or a shaft which goes vertically through the centre of the house and ends in a skylight, which illuminates nothing. Behind a panel in the wall of the shaft there is a room with a window, but no door. Normally, at this point, there are hints about concealed hiding places against religious persecution, but it is more likely to be due to the whims of landlords over the centuries.

There is a restaurant in the Elizabethan Long Gallery room, a Boswell Grill, and a modern touch, a barbecue built outside in the garden. At the Anchor one can wine and dine or just eat.

The Dr Johnson Room upstairs has a glass case which contains a first-edition of the famous lexicon; presumably a page is turned each day. A random selection under Discourse gave: *To reafon; to paff from premife to confequence.*

Outside a terrace has been built over the river and one can sit at a table to drink a pint of ale above the quay from where ships once transported prisoners – maybe from the Clink to Virginia or New South Wales – while enjoying one of the best views of London.

The Thames over the years has known pirates, smugglers and press-gangs and even the ship of a Dutch Admiral – Van Tromp – who sailed up the river with a broom at the peak to signify that he could sweep the British from the seas. In 1666, the customers at the old Anchor might have taken their pewter pots outside to witness the great fire of London redden the sky as the city burned across the water, not knowing that ten years later, it would be their turn when the whole Southwark would burn in an equally disastrous blaze.

The fine bow window of the Anchor would have been occupied in 1941, by customers watching the city burn with St Paul's silhouetted against the blaze, as the Luftwaffe tried to destroy it.

The narrow lanes of the present Bankside are no longer peopled with lusty apprentices prowling the alleys in search of a wench, or cat-calling the villain amongst the groundlings of the Globe Theatre. One is more likely to hear from a pleasure craft, the electronically boosted voice of boatman calling: "...the famous Anchor Inn..." But even if customs change, he is still the same type who once earned a living by the strength of his back as a waterman on the river. Like the

Anchor, he has changed to suit the needs of his customers, yet he remains a living history of the city of which the good doctor was wont to exclaim:

'Sir, he who is tired of London is tired of life.'

YE OLDE CHESHIRE CHEESE
145 Fleet Street, EC4

How to get there

There are streams of buses from Charing Cross: Nos. 4, 6, 9, 11, 15 going east. Get off at the Daily Telegraph building. The entrance to the pub is the tiny court called Wine Office Court, where Sir Walter Raleigh once had an office "To make lycences for keeping of taverns and retayling of wines". Oliver Goldsmith lived at No. 6 and wrote part of *The Vicar of Wakefield* there.

Ye Olde Cheshire Cheese may well be the most visited tavern on earth, but it remains a great pub genuinely steeped in the old English tradition. Its literary traditions alone reads like a scroll of fame. At one time or another in its 250 year old history, its customers have included: Dr Johnson, Boswell, Pope, Thackeray, Voltaire and Dickens.

Dr Johnson was a local who lived in adjacent Gough Square where he worked on his famous lexicon. He loved to be in the pub atmosphere – disputatious, perhaps, but always convivial. One can imagine him rolling down the alley to enter the narrow passageway and sit himself down on one of the oak pews beneath the black oak beams of the low ceiling in the tiny bar on the ground floor which would have made a good Forum for the display of his erudi- tion. Here in the stimulating company of Boswell or Garrick, the great actor of the time – a former pupil and great friend – he would hold forth, his voice a gale, reverberating in the confines of the tiny place. The perfect setting for Johnson but not for Oliver Goldsmith of whom Johnson remarked. "No man was more foolish when he hadn't a pen in his hand or more wise when he had", another patron of the time, a young painter named Joshua Reynolds, was also a member of the company.

THE OLD WATLING
29 Watling Street, EC4

How to get there
Underground (Central line) to St Paul's. From station walk east on Cheapside to the famous church of St Mary le Bow. Turn into Bow Lane, by the side of the church, and walk through into Watling Street.

As you walk down Bow Lane – there is a half timbered building on your left and the church wall towering above you – London will probably subject you to its famous trick of conjuring up a previous century. The snarl of the traffic on Cheapside appears to fall to a whimper and there is room only for a pedestrian in the lane. In the church spire above your head, the bells have become the subject of a London legend which says "A Cockney is anyone born within the sound of Bow bells".

When Sir Christopher Wren set about rebuilding London after the Great Fire of 1666, he made the rebuilding of St Mary le Bow an early project and recruited his team of artisans to start the work, but before he could start his men had to have some kind of shelter, so he erected the building which became The Old Watling.

Pubs are erected and dismantled, they change hands, they are altered to suit the breweries or individuals who own them, but not the Old Watling which, in appearance is a 17th century pub. Within, the dark oak panelling, the timber and plaster of the walls, the exposed roof beams, the dark oak tables and settles remain 17th century. It is as English as plum duff and – God willing – will remain so.

Like most City of London pubs it becomes a Local at lunchtime when the people from the local offices come in for their sandwich and pint of Real Ale, then, the big bar booms with the drone of local gossip, but, outside the hours of noon and say two thirty in the afternoon the place, particularly in the small back bar, is quiet. Its

Opening times are the usual 11am to 11pm at week- days but it closes early on Saturday evenings and does not open all day Sunday. Which is about standard in the City of London where people mainly go home to the suburbs every evening.

The atmosphere of the place lies in it, sense of continuity; through centuries it has served as a place where ordinary people have come for a bite and a drink and break from their jobs – refreshment in other words. It is really a monument to the ordinary block. If Sir Christopher Wren, England's greatest architect, has his monument up the road in St Paul's cathedral, the ordinary working block who humped the stones and hewed the beams, has his in a pub like The Old Watling. As I sat in the back contemplating this, a couple of Artisans from a neighbouring building site came through with their pints and began a game of darts.

THE FLASK
77 West Hill, Highgate, N6

How to get there
Underground to Archway station on the Northern line. From Archway station, walk up Highgate Hill, or take a Nᵒ· 210 bus to West Hill.

A traditional pub, the Flask has not only an ancient history, but is situated in the prettiest of the rural villages in the precincts of London that resist the creeping tide of sameness which has invaded the capital. Founded in 1663 with part of the original building still in existence, it is listed under the Act for the Preservation of Ancient Monuments (i.e. the Government protects the structure of the building from being altered on the whims of Landlords). Whether it was by edict of the Landlord or the appropriate Government department, the large area in front of the inn has not been turned into a car park . Tables are arranged where customers may sit in peace under the shade of ancient trees while enjoying home cooked English food and drinking real-ales.

The area was once called Hampstead Wells where people could drink of the Chalybeate waters which they believed to be beneficial to health. They would bring flasks to take the water home and it is from this custom that the inn draws its name. There is still something of a resort about the place but you cannot drink of the Chalybeate waters – the brewery provides it's own.

The building is arranged to form a kind of square to make it resemble a seventeenth century farmhouse. Inside, in keeping with its history, it is furnished with eighteenth century period pieces. At weekends there is something of a holiday atmosphere in the vicinity of the pub, although around the corner in Pond Square even the modern pest of cars cluttering the streets cannot hide it's elegance and one can sit beneath the trees which line it and dream of the famous people who may have sat there years ago. Men like Francis Bacon or Karl Marx (buried in Highgate Cemetery) who was fond of a pint and would have undoubtedly patronised The Flask. One can imagine him sitting in the courtyard of the pub arguing with his friend and collaborator Frederick Engels; laying down the tenets of The Socialist Manifesto. Many famous figures ranging from George Eliot to Herbert Spencer have lived here and the old folk-tale of Sir Richard Wittington who paused on Highgate Hill defeated, on his way home to the country, after failing to make his fortune, but turned back to become Lord Mayor of London, still delights the kids.

The main road to the North of England ran for centuries up Highgate Hill and The Flask must have witnessed many a traveller fortifying himself before making his assault on the capital.

THE TWO CHAIRMEN
Dartmouth Street, SW1

How to get there
Underground to St. James's Station (District or Circle line) Dartmouth St. is diagonally right from station.

The Two Chairmen, as the sign indicates, are Sedan chair bearers, not heads of committee. In 1756, when the pub was established, they would be the modern equivalent of cab drivers.

The pub hides itself modestly at the top of Dartmouth Street, where it curves into Old Queen Street. Lord Dartmouth, for whom the street is named, once lived hereabouts. The pub is on the site of the Royal Cockpit, shown in Hogarth's painting of the 'Blind Gambler', who was Lord Albemarle Bertie. You can get a fix on the pub from the following notice in the window.

'All the rights and interests of all the said assigned Inn to the beneficial agreement for the lease of a substantial Public House known by the name of the Dartmouth Arms or the Two Chairmen eligibly situate on the east side of Dartmouth Street Westminster now occupied by Mr Grosvenor on lease for a term of twenty years from Lady Day 1803.'

The Passport Office is a neighbour, and the lowing of tourists can almost be heard from nearby Westminster Abbey ... but the tourists do not come here, although the adjacent Queen Anne's Gate is a lovely example of eighteenth century building at its best.

Across the street the door of the Fabian Society, painted (appropriately) red, looks poverty-stricken. Its bookshop, where they once sold the pamphlets that radically changed post-war Britain, is now a 'caff', selling bangers and mash, rather than revolutionary ideas.

Inside The Two Chairmen, you get an instant impression of the coziness that is the hallmark of a good local. The dark oak panelling of the bar is lightened by brightly lit murals showing scenes of chairmen conveying passengers. Eighteenth century prints warm the effect of the dark panels. The oak settles have been arranged in alcoves to provide intimacy.

The clientele consists of well-dressed men taking their lunch breaks. Rather like City men, they chat animatedly, but, – perhaps due to the higher ceilings – the noise of their conversation is quite a few decibels lower.

There is a restaurant upstairs, again very cozy, but

of the 'entertaining-a-client-on-the-expense-account' kind. Downstairs at street level, they serve real-ales and baps filled with ham, beef or cheese.

At lunchtime, the Two Chairmen is a local for the professional people who work in the neighbourhood who want to eat with their colleagues in a very cozy atmosphere. In the evening, the pub would be very quiet.

The Cutty Sark

COVENT GARDEN

Covent Garden is not so much a topographical area as a way of life. Like the Left Bank, Greenwich Village, The Plaka, it invokes a sense of diving head first into Life! Slap bang in the centre of London, only a stone's throw from the Theatre District and the National Art Gallery, it harbours a nest of tiny streets and lies on the verge of what was once the 'Thieve's Kitchen of Seven Dials' where even 'Bow Street Runners' would not venture alone. It also contains Inigo Jones elegant piazza where the fruit and vegetable market used to be before it was moved to another site.

When it was a market, every square foot of the streets around would be covered by market produce or the trucks or carts of the farmers and vendors leaving no room for the market porters to wheel their barrows – so they had to resort to carrying baskets on their heads to take out the produce ... one could observe porters with as many as four or five bushel baskets balanced on their heads.

Under the vast glass dome of The Flower Market, Floral Hall, the air would be honey sweet with the scent of thousands of flowers waiting to be sold and in the Piazza. The Flower Gels, wrapped against the chill of winter would shuck peas or wire up wreaths or bunches of violets.

The Market pubs of those days fed the market porters with delicacies like fried gammon rashers and 'bubble and squeak' (fried cabbage and potatoes) washed down with pint pots of ale. Now the Piazza has been turned into a Tourist Area where 'buskers' (itinerant musicians) play to the wandering tourists as they feed at one of the many 'Caffs' or fast food places under the glass roofs of the Piazza. All the old pubs are still alive and kicking in Covent Garden and a new one called The Punch and Judy is on the site where the puppets were first introduced to England.

The old Cockney spirit is still very much in evidence, as witnessed from a balcony overlooking the Piazza. One of the old time flower gels with her wicker basket loaded, was watching a young couple approaching. When they arrived, she planted her basket at their feet so that they could hardly get around it.

"Vi-lets Sir. Luvly Vi-lets?"

The young man looked startled while the girl looked away. They would have turned away had the flower gel not held a bunch of violets against the girl's black coat.

"They go luvly with that coat, Sir ... 'ere!"

She thrust them into the hand of the girl,

"Take 'em luv, from me 'cos they look so nice!"

Naturally the young man rose to the occasion and paid double.

After a token resistance she accepted the money. As they walked away she called after them, "Gawd bless yer, Sir."

Covent Garden has always been the haunt of the man-about-town. When pubs sold more coffee than beer (a temporary phase), places like Will's would be patronised by Dryden who attended to hear the latest news and gossip.

The Coffee Houses were patronised by the middle- and upper-classes, but after such places became popular the elite retired to private clubs where one had to be elected as a member, thus leaving the pubs to provide a forum for those of a more democratic stamp.

The pubs in the Covent Garden area still attract lively and mainly young people who are in Covent Garden to attend the opera or theatre or who are just 'pub crawling' in the famous pubs there.

Covent Garden was the background for some of the scenes in the film of *My Fair Lady* and it was at The Globe in Bow Street that Hitchcock filmed a part of *Frenzy*.

With the Royal Opera House offering opera and the Theatre Royal offering theatre and the Lyceum offering such capers as Miss World beauty contests, Youth is at the helm and pleasure is at the prow in Covent Garden.

LAMB & FLAG
33 Rose Street, WC2

How to get there
Underground (Piccadilly line) to Covent Garden. From station turn left into Long Acre. Rose Street is the third turning on the left, going west.

There has been a pub of one kind or another here for 400 years. During the time when bare knuckle fights were held upstairs, the place was known to the cauliflower ear fraternity as 'The Bucket of Blood'. A modern Cabby still acknowledges the nickname.

On another bloody occasion, in the 17th century, the Poet Laureate, Dryden, who was a regular there, was set upon by thugs in the employ of Louise de Keronelle, a mistress of King Charles whose agent had sent them to 'do' Dryden for writing scurrilous verses about her. Dryden was nearly 'done' to death.

King Charles was of the opinion that: "God will never damn a man for allowing himself a little pleasure" but he had a somewhat majestic conception of what constitutes a little since he fathered 14 known bastards. In his out of bed moments, though, he made his presence known around Covent Garden since he initiated the Royal Opera house and the market's elegant piazza there. The picturesque market has been removed to a dreary site across the river but the piazza remains as a tourist attraction.

Undisturbed by these goings on in it's vicinity, the Lamb & Flag continued to remain vigorously alive by giving the public what it demands. In the 17th century the Lamb & Flag provided a meeting place for the wits of the town to meet and exchange the issues of the day whilst having fun. The atmosphere of the place – one traverses a narrow court to enter a smallish bar panelled in black oak, called the Dryden Bar, where the oak beams and coal fire burning in the grate, is reminiscent of Dryden's day. Even if the Media has taken over the communication of news more efficiently nowadays people still want to meet to have fun. There is always the buzz of high spirited discourse and laughter in the Lamb & Flag from the sort of people who are still young enough to express bold opinions.

Like Gwen and Winsome who squeezes up to make room for me at their table. They had come twelve thousand miles and were determined to see a pub. "Me Mum was born a Cockney" confided Gwen. "The one thing she missed in Australia was the pub. We have pubs back home but they aren't anything like this. The people here are different in pubs – they will talk, know what I mean?" Under the roar of multi conversations she felt emboldened to voice her thoughts, "Look at him". She pointed to a small man who sat is the corner of a settle. His face was painted a dead white and his eyebrows were blackened by grease paint, a small moustache was painted on his upper lip.

"Why is he dressed like Charlie Chaplin? See! the baggy trousers and the bowler hat that is too small?"

He heard and screwed his head round. "I'm a busker."

"What's a busker?"

"A street performer." He got up. "I have to go. My public are waiting for me." He gave Charlie's little lift of the hat and waggled off.

Gwen watched him pass through the crowd to the door giving the little lift of his bowler hat to acknowledge a pat on the back.

"That's London for you," commented Gwen.

There are other lowly practitioners of their art who perform in the streets surrounding the Lamb & Flag. Like the man who brings his piano on a truck. The man who tears old newspapers into intricate shapes, the spoon players, the violinist. There are even card tricksters. A more precarious trade these days now that Bobbies use Panda cars instead of patrolling the beat on the two flat feet. The Con Men have been driven to designing a table that can be folded in a flash and carried by a handle so that it looks like a portfolio of drawings. They complain self righteously about the cost of Pandas to the tax payer "A diabolical liberty, ain't it?"

The Lamb & Flag has the usual pub food but with places like Rule's and Simpson in the immediate neighbourhood they have heavy competition. When it comes to drinks their long lineage tells; they can serve you ancient drinks like Sack and a mulled ale. The continuity endures as in Dryden's day. It is a place where the bright and lively come to talk.

THE NAG'S HEAD
Corner of James Street and Floral Street, Covent Garden.

How to get there
Underground (Piccadilly line) to Covent Garden (closed on Sunday).

The pub is a relic of the days when the pubs of Covent Garden were mainly frequented by the market porters. In those days magistrates would grant concessions that allowed the porters to drink at gruesome hours, adjusted to the work of the market. Then it would be crowded with weather-beaten Cockneys, wearing leather aprons and padded headgear, necessary to carry bushel baskets on their heads. In raucous voices, suited to attract the attention of the customer to whom he was delivering his load of Brussels sprouts or whatever, he would call, "Nah Smiff! Let's 'av yer!'' – thirsty work, requiring a beer with a bit of strength in it. History has it that the beer called Porter was especially brewed for them. With his Porter, he would eat a two-eyed steak   a Kipper (smoked herring) – or bread and cheese with pickled onions or Picalilli (a fearsome concoction of cauliflower, onions, and chilies, all floating in a mustard sauce). Nowadays, the menu is more suited to the tourists who flock to the new Covent Garden, which is designed to amuse, or to the musically inclined, who come here for the Royal Opera House, which looms just across the road.

The Nag's Head sells real-ales and the usual pub grub. The small bars have been reduced to one large bar with alcoves. It is no longer a local, where everyone knows each other, but nevertheless, it is a busy boozer, not designed for those who want tranquillity, but full of people out on a spree.

If you are alone, you may amuse yourself by eaves-dropping on other people's conversation, which, of necessity, has to be carried on at a force-five level on the Beauford scale. Everyone seems to have fun at the Nag's Head.

THEATRE PUBS

Pub landlords have always been interested in new ways to please customers. They have used their big 'Club' rooms for exhibitions, contests and functions of all kinds: boxing matches, dancing, Friendly Societies, Thrift and Loan clubs or dance tournaments.

One of the most successful ventures was the free and easy sing song where a piano player encouraged customers to sing the songs of the day. These became more elaborate when they attracted amateurs yearning to have their talents recognised. As the popularity of these shows increased landlords built stages for the performer sand sooner or later amateur impresarios presented themselves as Chairman or Master of Ceremonies. This office required someone of dominant personality who could not only control the temperament of the 'artistes' but could deal with the audience in a voice which would flatten a gale. A thick skin was also a requirement of the office since it had to be a s thick as an elephant's to withstand the shafts hurled at it by the audience.

The Chairman had his chair set in some place close to the stage where he could act as link between the stage and audience. His instrument of office was a gavel which he whacked on a block to get attention before introducing the next 'Turn' in immodest terms such as "Ladies & Gentlemen! I have the honour to introduce Madame Olga! Give the little lady a hand please! Madame Olga has appeared before all the crowned heads of Europe!" He would then pause to ride out the storm of cat calls that were a time honoured part of the festivities before resuming, "Madame Olga has consented to cancel an important engagement to sing for her favoured audience."

These concerts were so successful that they attracted the attention of the professionals. Thus Music Hall, or Vaudeville, was born. Mister Chairman became an Impresario who would take over a theatre and call it a Music Hall in order to show what was called Variety – in America,

Vaudeville. Charlie Chaplin started his career at Gatti's theatre in London.

There was not the abundance of amusements in those days and the stars toured with the same act word for word for years. Nevertheless, they were idolised.

Music Hall withered and died when Cinema took over and Cinema in it's turn, was hard hit by Television. Now, Variety is being reborn in the pubs of London.

Playwrights have seen a great opportunity, too, to break the hold of the agents by producing their own plays in pubs. There are scores of pubs in London where one can see anything from a satirical revue, through a Problem play to a comedy.

The revolt has spread to the actors who, tired of being on the dole for half of their lives, are performing in pubs – in any vehicle including the classics of Ibsen, Kafka and Shaw.

THE WATER RATS
328 Grays Inn Rd, WC1

How to get there
Underground to King's Cross station (Northern, Piccadilly or Victoria lines). From station cross Euston Road into Grays Inn Road and walk (5 mins) south to pub on left hand side of Grays Inn Rd.

This well known pub used to be called The Pindar of Wakefield. Now the Abadaba company of professional actors have taken over the entertainment and made it into the premier music hall pub in central London. Once a sprawling Victorian pub with the elaborate furnishings of that era, it has been remodelled to contain a cosy restaurant where you may eat dinner before the curtain goes up then remain in your seat to enjoy the show.

The sort of entertainment provided is very much of the Victorian Variety type, with a Master of Ceremonies to introduce the acts and narrate the story which could be a melodrama with a wicked squire, an innocent young girl, a baby left on a doorstep and the wicked squire getting his come-uppance in the last act. The M.C. quickly establishes direct contact with the audience and is not above interrupting the story on the slightest pretext to indulge in repartee or to encourage the audience to boo or hiss the villain. It is great fun!

After the show, the actors mingle with the audience. You have the opportunity to chat and buy them a drink. They look smaller and more ordinary off stage, but it engenders a feeling of being part of the show. After all, you did hiss and boo!

Music Hall is performed Thursday to Saturday around 8 pm. If you wish to book a table for dinner, you may telephone beforehand. Otherwise you just take in your drink. There is an extension of the bar into the auditorium in case your throat becomes dry with all the booing. Gate money is charged to non diners.

When the repertory players are not performing, music, usually jazz, is performed.

THE KING'S HEAD
115 Upper Street, Islington, N1

How to get there
Underground (Northern line) to The Angel. From station turn right then right again into Islington High Street then on to Upper Street. The King's Head is on the left, going north.

The King's Head is the Old Vic of the Pub/Theatre world. It doesn't merely show plays it explores the gamut of theatre from Stringberg to Cockney comediennes. In the Fall it promotes a festival where you may see shows directly from the Edinburgh Festival. Examples taken from past programs include a comedy from Poland, a standup comedian, a dream play by Strindberg, *The Outsider* by Camus (presented by Royal Academy of Dramatic Art) and many more including a cabaret.

The evening show starts at 8.00pm and a late night show at 11-30; there is also a lunch time show at 1.15pm. To quote the *Sunday Telegraph*, ''These vivacious, witty shows have become the speciality of this Little Theatre.''

The King's Head has a well equipped kitchen that allows it to serve full course dinners. You may remain to enjoy the show after your meal. It also has a barbecue where they will make you a Hamburger to order.

With all this, the King's Head remains essentially a pub. A typical Victorian pub with lighted fires in the large, U-shaped bar which is very large but not too large to accommodate the crowd. At about 9.00pm a grand piano is played by on of those drifters whose accent ranges from Deep South when he is playing blues to Jamaica when he is into Reggae. When he takes off the cowboy's hat he effects, his head appears shiny as a billiard ball. He is a character and the customers crowd round him and beseech him to play the stuff of their dreams. They are a cosmopolitan crowd. Walk along Upper Street and you will find restaurants that specialise in a score of different ethnic foods to cater to the emigrants of a score of different nations. For some reason there has always been a large body of Cypriots both of Greek and Turkish origin. It has always been a district favoured by political refugees. Islington has sheltered Lenin, Marx and Engels. It is one of the few areas in London that could support a pub with so varied a programme of plays. The cosmopolitan atmosphere may attract the roamers who are always on the way to somewhere else – looking for the good life. They are an articulate crowd who do not stand on ceremony, who will offer their opinions to the nearest person. Before there was a national theatre in London, Islington supported The Sadlers Wells theatre which was the home of The British Opera and Ballet. Whatever the King's Head is it is not dull. The cosmopolitan nature of the residents ensures this.

ALMEIDA WINE BAR
Almeida Street, Islington, N1

How to get there
Underground (Northern line to Euston – change for Angel) from Angel station turn right into Islington High Street then right again into Upper Street. Walk north on Upper Street (10 mins) to Almeida Street on left.

This is a wine bar attached to a theatre but with a side entrance. One does not have to go to the theatre; access to the bar is through a courtyard with whitewashed walls that have plants or vines creeping over them. Lamps in elegant wrought iron brackets light the walls. The effect is of sunlight warming the wall of some bodega in the Mediterranean. A bicycle propped against the wall gives a homely touch. A line of washing is the only missing prop. The entrance to the bar is on one side of the courtyard and the entrance to the theatre on the other. In the bar, a piano and saxophone provide background music for a young, nicely dressed crowd seated at small tables. The atmosphere is that of a French cafe with the waiter and Patron (struggling actors?) giving excellent performances. There is a limited wine list and wine can be ordered by the glass or the bottle.

A pleasant place to take your guest after the theatre. One doesn't have to bother with the car or coats when only a stroll across the courtyard is all that is required to spend a pleasant hour over a bottle of wine and a snack.

The theatre favours Shakespeare's plays. They are excellently performed by a resident company.

CROWN & WOOLPACK
St John's Street, EC1

How to get there
Underground to Angel station (Northern line) From station cross road to St John's Street. Walk (3 mins) South passing Old Red Lion to Crown & Woolpack on left.

Of thousands in the mile-long queue to see Lenin's body in the Kremlin how many would have heard of the Crown & Woolpack? Yet it was at the Crown & Woolpack, in the room over the big bar that the exiled Lenin conspired to overthrow the Czar; here that he held meetings of the Bolshevik cell whose members were destined to become powerful in a communist government.

In 1902 Lenin lived in Holford square, a few minutes away from the Crown & Woolpack. A great deal of his time was given up to Iskra the Russian language newspaper he produced in Clerkenwell Green. At meetings of the cell in a room above the big bar he would read extracts from Iskra. In this same room nowadays, every night at 8-30pm, one can watch the plays of struggling authors unfold their plots, although none so audacious as the plot to take over a country stretching from the Baltic to the Bering seas. Many pubs have provided footnotes to history but none so contemporary. A framed copy of a newspaper cutting located in the big bar downstairs, relates the story.

There has been a pub on the site since 1797. In the days when highway men were a menace it became known as a place to wait for other travellers going north to make up a convoy for protection. The tradition has persisted since others have sought protection. In the political field, notably, Karl Marx as well as Lenin.

Today the pub is a bright, cheerful place. The many partitions that formed it into small bars have been removed – except for the one which divides the Saloon bar from the big bar; this makes it necessary to go out into the street to pass from one bar to the other.

The small theatre has to face severe competition from another theatre pub almost next door and from Sadler's Wells, the famous theatre just down the road. Its modest charges may have something to do with that.

ARGYLE ARMS
18 Argyle Street, Oxford Circus, W1

How to get there
Tube to Oxford Circus (Bakerloo Line) The pub is a few yards from the station on the corner of Oxford Street and Argyle Street.

The Argyle is a pub famous for its association with theatre world. A large, lively example of the Victorian era with its separate bars, its lovely old acid-etched mirrors, its mahogany woodwork, its bosomy barmaids and its air of confidence which implies "This is the place where it's all going on". Its fortunes have always been tied with that of the Palladium theatre across the street which reached a zenith in the thirties when The Crazy Gang were playing at the theatre. It took a war to stop The Crazy Gang but the pub went on through war time blackouts, bombing, and shortages of every kind. Playing the Palladium was the equivalent of an Oscar in the acting profession. Old Timers may sometimes be seen in the pub – sitting on a stool by the Argyle Street entrance – disparaging the talents of the moderns.

The pub is beloved of Americans. The phrase "Playing at the Palladium is something a New Yorker, at least, will understand and while I was there an American flashed photographs. The snack bar provides Club sandwiches of American proportions and a refrigerator held the main American beers served "ice cold". Not that the owners are trying to alter the atmosphere of the pub, quite to the contrary. The Victorian atmosphere is emphasised. A huge mirror in scarlet and gold which covers one wall is quite a work of art. A hop bine rooted in a large tub trails live hops over it then goes on up to the moulded ceiling. The original mahogany partitions which segregated the different bars into small or large boxes with names like Snug, Ladies, Bottle and Jug Public and Saloon are still there but without doors. One enters a long passage lined with mirrors and ambles along it perusing each bar in turn to decide which to enter.

Mount the broad staircase and the hustle of the ground floor is muted to a totally different atmosphere. It is determinedly Victorian still but with secluded alcoves dimly lit by lights made to resemble gas lamps whose light reflected on the panels of mahogany which line the alcoves bring up a sheen on the polished surface. Heavy plush curtains frame wide windows that look down on the lighted street lamps of Argyle Street. Alcoves always suggest people who want to be secluded. These give an impression of waiting. A young woman reads from a sheaf of typewritten papers, a young man looks down into Argyle Street then glances at his watch. A middle aged man hurries in and greets the young woman. They become absorbed in the papers. I indulge in the exercise of assigning them parts in a scenario – an exercise which becomes pleasantly habitual in the lone pub watcher

– but good manners demand that I do not watch overtly. Outside the front door some long gone person has indulged in the Londoner's incurable habit of planting, in any odd corner, something that will summon nature to adorn. A species of ivy climbs from a tub and has twined itself around the front door. There is only pedes- trian traffic allowed in Argyle Street which allows of a place – lighted with golden globes I notice – which takes the overflow from the pub in the busy season. The absence of Wheeled traffic is pleasant – a barrow boy selling fruit doesn't count since he, or his type, have pushed their barrows through the crowded streets of London's "West End" for centuries. Before The Crazy Gang came to the Palladium even.

THE BEAR & STAFF
37 Charing Cross Road, WC1

How to get there
Underground (Northern line) to Leicester Square station. The pub is 2 minutes walk south on Charing Cross Road. It is opposite Windham's theatre; bus Nos 24,29,124,176, go along Charing Cross Road.

This is a theatre pub from way back. In the old days the pub used to be on what the cabbies called 'Poverty Corner' because of the unemployed actors who frequented it after a visit to "My Agent" on the opposite side of the street which had as many agents as a dog has fleas.

To the eavesdropper with appreciative ears and eyes, the pub was a free source of entertainment. One bought a pint; made oneself unobtrusive and tuned into the talk – there was no ear-strain either because they were all trained to make themselves audible at the back of the gallery; being actors, they loved an audience anyway. As they talked they changed character; becoming for a moment a mean landlady in some Macclesfield digs, an Irish train guard complaining "Sure! tis only fish and actors that travel on The Lord's Day", or reminisce about the time they played the Hippodrome at Huddersfield "The missus was preggers and here! She had to go and sing a song called "Grow little mushroom Grow".

That was a different era, now the pub itself has become the theatre and the actors no longer pass the time of day at the bar but work upstairs at the theatre where you take your drink with you upstairs and watch the professionals of the Arnaud Company perform every lunch time and evening. If you are pushed for time you can grab a pizza at a place a minute away – it used to be The Garrick pub – and across the road there is a small Caff where they sell hot beef sandwiches. The old time Artistes would curl up and die at the astonishing range of plays offered by the Arnaud company at the Bear & Staff. These modern actors perform anything from modern comedy to Kafka. At the Bear and Staff they do it twice a day – at 1.00pm and 8.00pm. They have laid the ghost of 'Poverty Corner'.

RIVER PUBS

Before London's docks were built, ship's anchored out in the stream. Access to them was by boat from one or other of the stairs such as Wapping Old Stairs. Pubs would locate as near to the stairs as possible. The only way out of the country was by ship and those who were anxious to find a ship would come to the pubs to enquire about a passage. Masters would come to sign on a crew at pubs also. The adventurers, even the colourful villains, who thronged the taverns of the 17th and 18th century are remembered by the taverns they frequented along the lower reaches of the river Thames – the gateway to high adventure in the countries beyond the seas.

By contrast, the pubs on the upper reaches of the river, have led a more sheltered existence. Picturesquely situated on the same river Thames which here flows limpidly clear through lush meadows, they have always been a source of pleasure, part of a day's outing of boating and fishing for Londoners. A place where the locals could drink beer while watching the antics of the pleasure craft on the river.

THE MAYFLOWER
117 Rotherhithe Street, SE16

How to get there
Underground (District line) to Whitechapel, then East London line to Rotherhithe. From station walk down Railway Avenue to Rotherhithe Street.

This is a riverside pub unique on two counts: it is the only pub allowed to break the Post Office monopoly to sell stamps and it is the starting place of the historical voyage of the Mayflower. According to the owners of the Mayflower pub which in 1620 was called The Shippe, Captain Christopher Jones, master and part owner of the 180-ton ship *Mayflower*, was "quaffing a pint of ale in the Shippe when he learned of his next assignment." As history recalls it was to take a party of colonists called Pilgrims to the "New World" (America).

Jones lived in Rotherhithe and berthed his ship close to the pub. As was the practice in those days he would have signed on his crew in the tavern. Jones was an interesting character who gossip said had been a pirate at some time in his career, but this was proved to be false. Somewhat shamefaced, after 320 years the authorities recognised Jones' valiant efforts on behalf of the Colonists when they placed a plaque on the wall of St Mary's church – just across the street from the pub – where Jones lies buried. They should have put the plaque in the pub.

Jones was buried in the churchyard of St Mary's but don't search for the tombstone for a part of the churchyard was asphalted over to provide a playground for children and their nimble feet now prance over the bones of Christopher Jones. Not a bad epitaph!

The Mayflower, once the Shippe, has over the centuries, been used by the watermen who could tie up their skiffs to it. At a later period – before the Surrey Docks were abandoned – dockers made it their local. There is something nautical about the interior of the pub. Ceilings are higher than they would have been in the 17th century but looking through the wide window that lets on to a deck over the river, one sees an occasional ship or tug working the tideway. It is not difficult to imagine being aboard a ship of 60ft by 15ft beam. Not that there are any affectations – just honest oak tables in panelled alcoves.

The owners have resisted the temptation to cover the walls with bits and pieces of brasswork. There is a framed document written in the angular characters of 1686, which portrays the last will and testament of a local woman named Beatrice Browning who bequeathed to Mary Sherwood, "The Shippe Inn behind the church of St Mary in Rother-hithe".

The abandonment of the docks has left Rotherhithe with a "has-been" look. A deserted village only a couple of miles downstream from London Bridge and the fretful energy of the city. The deserted warehouses with their rusting cranes will be snapped up by some developer soon.

The pub has a restaurant upstairs and there is pub lunch in the bar or visitors can take their bread and cheese out on to the veranda built over the river. One can look upstream to the Lower Pool, as the stretch of river between Tower Bridge and Limehouse Reach is known. The river has seen Viking Long Ships, Roman galleys, Clipper ships from China and P&O liners. It was the front line in the Battle of Britain. It provides a panorama of London's history.

THE TOWN OF RAMSGATE
62 Wapping High Street, E1

How to get there
By Underground (District line) to Whitechapel then change on to the East London line to Wapping station. Turn left out of station and continue (10mins) along Wapping High Street to Wapping Stairs. The pub is adjacent to the stairs.

The pub has seen some high adventure in its time. It was here that Captain Blood – who had stolen the Crown Jewels – was apprehended as he tried to make a getaway to some – any – foreign strand. Here too, the infamous judge Geoffreys stayed strictly incognito as he waited for a ship. Geoffreys was King James' Lord Chief Justice. At the 'Bloody Assizes' – where he sentenced 300 to death and 800 to be transported to the 'Colonies' – he proved to be a savage bully who ridiculed defendants accused of plotting against the King. When James was overthrown, Geoffreys decided that a trip abroad would be good for his health. Dressed as a sailor, he waited at the Town of Ramsey. Trusting to his disguise, he allowed himself to be seen in the bar, but he was recognised by one who had suffered at his hands. He was nearly lynched by the crowd but some soldiers rescued him and took him to the nearby Tower of London where, eventually, he died.

The pub really looks the part of a 17th century tavern. No attempt has been made to embellish it; it looks what it was then; a tavern where seamen hung out in the

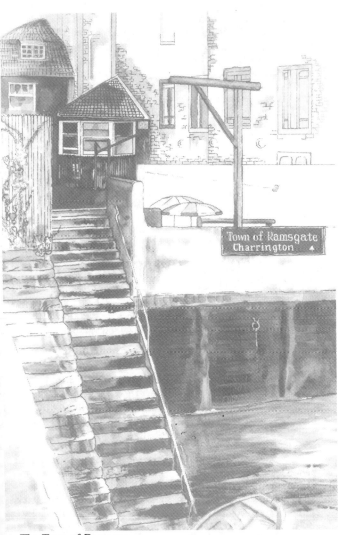

The Town of Ramsgate.

was then; a tavern where seamen hung out in the far off days of sail. Naturally it no longer has the air of tension – the whispering and plotting of its more adventurous days. On the wall cartoons of Hogarth do something to recall them but the atmosphere is down right matey and music lightens the air. There is a veranda overlooking the river where you can sit as Doré once sat to sketch the river close to Wapping Old Stairs where the 'Grace of Wapping' was once conveyed – it consisted of hanging a man in chains while three tides washed over him.

In the days of tall ships with clouds of sails, Wapping was a bustling place. The ships would anchor out in the stream and the watermen's skiffs would be sculling to and fro. Nowadays one is more like to see a pleasure boat man at the microphone than a sturdy waterman heaving on the scull as he fights a four knot tide to reach a ship bound for Valparaiso or Halifax.

PROSPECT OF WHITBY
57 Wapping Wall, E1

How to get there
Underground (District line) to Whitechapel change to the East London line to Wapping station. Turn right out of station and walk east along Wapping High Street (10mins).

This pub has a gruesome distinction – it overlooks the site of the old Execution Dock. In 1701, the notorious pirate Captain Kidd had The Grace of Wapping conferred upon him here. It con- sisted of hanging the felon in chains while three full tides washed over him. In those more robust days such spectacles were fixed to take place during public holidays. One can imagine the scene in the Prospect: the flagstone floor swimming in spilt beer, the boarded ceiling echoing with raucous laughter.

The boarded ceiling with blackened beams; the pewter counter, propped up by barrels to support its great weight; and the stone flagged floor are all still there, just as they were when the indefatigable Pepys condescended to participate

The Prospect of Whitby.

in the proceedings. The upstairs dining room is dedicated to him.

How they ate in those days! Oysters, not by the dozen but by the barrel and, according to a menu quoted by the Brewery, morsels like "A good calves head boiled with dumplings, fruit tart and cheese and, of course, plenty of wine of all sorts."

In the days when the World was largely unknown, 'The Prospect' was the hangout of adventurers yearning to make their fortune; but in 1553 when Sir Hugh Willoughby went there to raise a crew it was for the purpose of discovering the north-east passage to China. He never did find it and his voyage ended in disaster.

In later days the pub became known for its sporting propensities. It staged bare-knuckle fights and it also had a cockpit.

It must have been the river that attracted such artists as Turner, who at times lived there. Turner's best known painting 'The Last Voyage of the Fighting Temeraire' was painted when the ship was towed to a Breaker's Yard across the river at Rotherhithe.

Since it was first opened as 'The Devil' in 1543 – it was renamed more respectably after a Newcastle collier in 1790 – the pub has known the bold, the adventurous, the famous and the infamous. Judge Geoffreys lived nearby in Butcher's Row and would sometimes drop in to watch the executions at Execution Dock. As the judge of the 'Bloody Assizes' he was responsible for the provision of what may be called the 'raw material' for these executions. The Prospect's fame extends beyond the shores of England. The arrival of a coach-load of foreigners is not unusual. The Dutch ran a shipping line to Batavier from a dock nearby and the seamen became regulars for some years. Other regulars were the crews of Thames sailing barges – but as these crews consisted only of of a man, a boy and a dog, the Landlord could not exactly get fat on the barge trade. Nowadays, he would hardly get fat on the local trade either, since the docks were closed down and Wapping became a ghost town; but in the summer the imaginative still come attracted by its past history.

CITY BARGE
Strand on the Green, Chiswick, W4

How to get there
British Rail from Waterloo to Kew Bridge. Cross main road and walk to the towpath to Strand on the Green. Walk almost to the railway bridge over the River Thames.

This pub might have been A.P. Herbert's local. It has low ceilings with wooden beams from which ancient beer mugs hang. There is a brick fireplace with a cast iron grate. High shelves around the plaster and beamed walls hold dishes that were made by some potter, who, had he been alive now, would top the century. One can sit at deal tables to enjoy a ploughman's lunch that can be served with half-dozen varieties other than cheese. It is excellent and not expensive. The beer is Courage and Foster's lager.

One approaches the pub from a walk along the towpath where ancient willows line the path, in places arching overhead. Sitting at a table outside the pub, with a view of the mighty Thames, here reduced to a limp stream, flowing past a tree-covered island, you enjoy a scene far removed from the rush and roar of Chiswick, W4. A smiling young barmaid, on walkabout from Australia, pulls up a pint of Foster's lager, which has become a big seller in London. She explains about the lunch and I order a Ploughman's of beef, with crisp salad, which includes pickled onions.

The customers are mixed – the pub is quite well-known and includes visitors, but also an knot of locals who are celebrating the return of their pub at the tail-end of the tourist season. They obviously come from one of the row-houses, expensively converted, with names like Magnolia Cottage – which run along the river towpath.

Strand on the Green is not a name dreamed up by developers. It is genuine once-sleepy village. Now the transport facilities of rail and road have been brought to the boundaries, but it still remains one of the villages of London, maybe washed by the flotsam and jetsam of nearby Chiswick, but remaining a tiny enclave of rural charm.

CITY PUBS

On the site of an ancient gate of the city, Temple Bar delineates the jurisdiction of the City of London from the old City of Westminster where the King had his palace.

The powerful City Guilds split with Charles 1 because he abrogated some of their privileges. To show that they meant business in the protection of their interests the guilds of the City of London raised trained bands who were armed. Even Today the Lord Mayor of London, who is elected by the Guilds, governs the city east of Temple Bar; he still has his own regiment – The Honourable Artillery Company – and his own police force.

When the Queen pays a ceremonial visit to the City, she goes through a token ceremony of stopping at Temple Bar to request permission to enter the Lord Mayor's territory. Vice-versa, the Lord Mayor asks permission of the Crown – represented by the Lord Chief Justice – when he makes a ceremonial visit to the City of Westminster. It is all very polite. This is the way City people are, they represent the wealth of the country and they want the Crown, especially, to know it.

There is an air of old money about the narrow streets and courts of the city. Where every square foot of earth is worth it's weight in gold, the Guilds are apt to squander it on a garden planted with trees and flowers between the towering buildings. They engage a company of Her Majesty's guards – visibly armed – to guard the Bank of England each day presumably because their own regiment is too busy making money.

The banks and financial houses still sport signs like the three brass balls of the Lombards. They maintain window boxes of flowers vivid with colour. The men who stroll about the streets wear good suits and sometimes their ties proclaim an exclusive school or club.

Age is no crime in the City and most of the buildings are massively old although of late years there has been significant rebuilding. The old days when a gentleman's word was his bond and a deal was consummated by a smack of the hand may well be out in this computer age, but men still meet for lunch in the City's pubs. Even women are now invading the pubs for lunch.

City pubs are in the same mode as other City institutions, the building may be old – even ramshackle – but the cuisine is above reproach. Wines, beer and food are of the best and even if the bar is in a cellar the fittings are elegant.

THE CITY F.O.B.
Lower Thames Street

How to get there
Underground (District line) to Monument station. From the station walk as though you were going to cross the bridge (2mins) watch for a flight of stone steps, on your left, and descent them to Lower Thames Street. Across the street you will see a church – St Magnus the Martyr. The F.O.B. is next door to the church.

In case you are in doubt, F.O.B. is a shipping term which means free on board. It would have been more appropriate to have had a more fishy title since until a few years ago, Billingsgate fish market stood on the site. It has now moved downstream to the Isle of Dogs. The porters of the market wore quaint flat topped hats made of wood, on which they carried boxes of fish. They were noted for their coruscating language which appears in the Oxford dictionary under Billingsgate. The fishmongers were always a rough lot. A fishmonger named William Walworth became Lord Mayor of London. Confronted by a huge crowd of rebel peasants in 1381 he, almost single handed, broke up the revolution by stabbing to death Watt Tyler, the rebels leader. He was knighted by Richard II and consequently accorded the privilege of lending Richard much money on future occasions. The dagger that Walworth used to stab Tyler is preserved in Fishmongers Hall – just across the street from the City F.O.B.

The neighbourhood is rich in history. The Monument which is just behind the Underground station, was erected by Sir Christopher Wren, to mark the spot where the Great Fire of London started.

The F.O.B.'s next door neighbour, St Magnus church, was also built by Wren to replace the original church which was burnt down in the fire. St Magnus sees a procession of Fishmongers each year, each man carrying a nosegay of flowers, come to pay tribute. The church's most famous official was Miles Coverdale who was the first to translate the whole Bible into English.

The F.O.B. contributes no historical links to the past but insists upon maintaining the ancient traditions of England. Crouched under the structure of London Bridge, it is a cellar, arched and panelled in black oak with settles along the walls and wine casks placed decoratively on the sawdust covered floor. It could very well be a 17th century tavern.

The owners refer to it as a "Traditional old English Ale and Port house that offers the best food and drink procurable". There is a "hand Raised Pie, or hot smoked English sausages, a mature Stilton, a Game Pie (lead shot hazard) or a Double Gloucester". The cheese and sausages are served with cottage bread and butter. The ham is cut from the bone. In the drinks line one can have English Ale from the cask such as Davey's Old Wallop either in a pint tankard, or a half gallon tankard. Natu- rally the wine is from

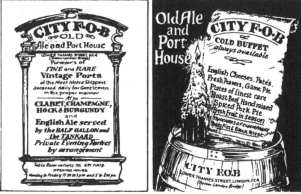

A card from the City FOB.

a cask; for example, take cask number eight which is a fine old tawny port you may buy by the pint mug, the house insists that if you are ordering a vintage port you must give twenty four hours notice for it to be properly decanted.

Apart from the range of wines that reads like an atlas, esoteric concoctions such as Black Velvet (a mixture of champagne and stout) by the tankard or Buck's Fizz.

The house makes every effort to make the place resemble a gentleman's club. There is a soberly dressed, butler who opens the door and wishes you "Good morning, Sir." At one minute after noon the greeting is changed to "Good afternoon Sir". When business becomes brisk, he will find you a table. If not – he wouldn't dream of seating you at a table with a stranger – he asks, reluctantly, may I suggest you sit at the bar, Sir?" It is all very civilised; nothing slap dash; everything of the best at the F.O.B.

THE OLD WINE SHADES
6 Martin Lane, EC4

How to get there
Underground to Monument Station (District line). Walk west along Cannon Street (2 minutes) to Martin Lane on left. The pub is on right by the junction with Arthur Street.

This place is right out of Dickens with it's authentic period front which contains an Off Licence which sells wine to take out. El Vino's, who own it, claim it to be the oldest wine house in London.

Inside there are chairs and tables that look like antiques and wood settles in panelled alcoves. The low ceilings are apt to darken a place; a consequence avoided by building a glass roof over the part that serves as a restaurant. You had better book for lunch since it is very popular with businessmen.

The Old Shades is such an institution that, some years ago when closure threatened, a public outcry was raised, successfully, to protect it.

The food is of the traditional English type of the best. The clientele are almost exclusively City men dressed in good suits; they are hearty and well nourished – particularly on the drinks side – and obviously don't have to worry about from where the next meal will be coming.

The Old Wine Shades is an institution as British as cricket. The only threat to its existence may be that the lifestyle which includes a hearty meal and drinks in the middle of the day may not be attuned to the computer age. Like most City pubs it is closed at weekends.

BILL BENTLEY'S WINE BAR
18 Old Broad Street.

How to get there
Underground to Bank Station (Northern or Central lines). From station cross road junction to Threadneedle Street. Walk east leaving Stock Exchange on left, to Old Broad Street. Bill Bentley's is on right, opposite to Stock Exchange.

Perhaps it is the heady influence of the Stock Exchange just across the street that gives the place the atmosphere of being at the hub of things. It is a tiny place but opulent, it has a bar at ground floor level and one below ground. There are small alcoves panelled in gleaming wood which reflects the discreet lighting. Downstairs there is a small dining room which can be shut off by sliding doors to hold a private party all squeezed together as in a boat.

The restaurant specialises in fish – both the fleshy kind and the crustacean – and one can indulge in such luxuries as caviar and smoked salmon washed down with Black Velvet (champagne and stout) beloved of Victorian actresses.

None of Bill Bentley's customers appears to be skint; even a brace of girls will drop in to split a bottle of Bubbly or something else selected from a wine list that reads like the Almanac de Gotha.

There is nothing lacking in the place except space – yet there is a small garden whose real estate value must be somewhere in the region of a pound sterling a square inch in this Tom Tiddler's Ground with neighbours like the Bank of England.

A card from Bill Bentley's.

The sporting propensities of the Regulars are represented by a racing skiff slung from the rafters under the glass roof of a sort of veranda.

The place is geared to the lifestyle of the old fashioned type of Stockbroker who wore a top hat and sealed bargains – handwritten on a pad – with a handshake.

Bentley's trade is virtually finished by 3.00pm and with the evening trade hardly worth bothering about, they close at 8.00pm. They remain closed on Saturdays and Sundays too.

JAMAICA WINEHOUSE
15 St Michael's Alley, Cornhill, EC3

How to get there
Underground to Mansion House District or Circle lines)
From station walk east on Cornhill to St Michael's Alley. The entrance is an inconspicuous door on the left.

Inside you will find a pub where, under the low ceilings formally dressed City men sit at dark oak tables or settles, drinking beer rather than wine in spite of the bar's original title which was styled before the Great Fire of London in 1666.

The memorable thing about the place is that the last link in the chain of history of the trade's development in the City. To quote a booklet put out by E.J. Rose, the owner, it is on the site of Pasqua Rose's Coffee House where 'The coffee drink was first publiquely made and sold in England'. Pasqua was a Greek brought to England to serve coffee to the public as a drink. The Great Fire of London destroyed the Coffee House but it was re-established as a place where underwriters wrote policies.

Knowing your average Englishman who is always ready to join hospitality with trade, it became a tavern. Before the Royal Mail took care of such matters, letters could be addressed to individuals, 'in care of The Jamaica Winehouse in St Michael's Alley'. Nowadays City men still drop in to get the latest information on what is happening on 'change, which covers everything from the latest cricket scores to the latest jokes. Voices boom under the low ceilings and conversations overheard are inclined to be flippant except at times of National crisis. There is a tradition in the City to serve in the Territorial forces. The City's Honourable Artillerie Company is a volunteer regiment. Framed and hung on the wall for historical reasons, a poster invites Royal Tars of old England to meet with W. Stevens at his rendezvous, Shoreham. Bounty will be given. Let us who are Englishmen protect and defend our King, George III!'

The Jamaica Winehouse is a good place to meet the 'Common, or Garden' Middle Class Englishman who is likely to wear a rose – grown in his own garden – in his buttonhole.

SAMUEL PEPYS
Brook's Wharf. Upper Thames Street, WC4

How to get there
British Rail to Cannon Street. From station turn left and first left (Dowgate) on to Upper Thames Street, turn east and walk (5 minutes) going East to Brook's Wharf. The pub is in a narrow lane that ends at the river.

The warehouse from which the pub has been created is more historic than the pub, but the architect did a wonderful job by leaving the original brick walls and ceilings intact, merely painting the arched ceilings and edging the supporting columns with a fine wood. Huge windows look out over the river – would you believe it for EC4? – framed by wisteria. The broad sweep of the river can be seen with every kind of craft: police launches, barges, pleasure steamers and tugs. London, while sprucing itself up for tourists, is also discovering itself for Londoners.

The restaurant at the Samuel Pepys is pricey, but worth it for the view alone. The clientele in the restaurant seems to be well-heeled – or on expense accounts. The food is excellent.

Class-consciousness still rears its ugly head in the shape of a large bar downstairs with brick walls and oak benches and settles designed for the people who work in the area – few people live there. Here they serve the usual pub food and real-ales. The atmosphere is noisy and matey, unlike the upstairs atmosphere, which is stilted and, as the wine takes effect, pompous.

The staff are quiet, deft and attentive: to give an example, they went to great lengths to protect two diners from the sun streaming through the window rather than asking them to move to another table.

As a City pub, the Samuel Pepys is closed at weekends.

THE WOOLPACK
Finch Lane (behind The Royal Exchange)

How to get there
Underground (District or Circle line) to Bank station. From station exit walk two or three minutes to the rear of the Exchange.

If you should enter any of the pubs close to a trading centre, you will encounter a roar of excited voices which carry over from it to adjacent pubs. This fact of life is very apparent vis-a-vis the Royal Exchange and the Woolpack since the entrance to the pub is a few steps from the

Exchange's back door. Venturing downstairs finds one in an atmosphere reminiscent of Henley rowing regatta – since the people there are apparently wearing the sort of blazers that the rowing fraternity affect at Henley. They are brightly coloured and designed to attract attention. The difference is that the blazers worn in Exchange have a trading company's name emblazoned across them. In front, prominently displayed, is the badge which allows the wearer to enter into the Exchange. These, mainly young men, come in to the pub not only to eat and drink but to share the excitement of the morning's trading, thereby maintaining an important function of a pub – socialising.

At lunchtime the Woolpack serves sandwiches or Ploughman's lunch – they also offer a very good real-ale.

The pub's name derives from the wool trade; a woolpack is a measure of wool, weighing roughly, two hundred and forty pounds which is a unit of the trade. The name of the seat upon which the Chancellor of the Exchequer is seated when in the House of Commons is known as the Woolsack. There must be some connection.

The Woolpack keeps early hours on weekdays and is closed at weekends. One does not go to pubs like the Woolpack for glitter – it has kept it's fittings and fixtures for what looks like centuries. They give it an atmosphere of continuity.

GUILD
Basinghall Street, EC2

How to get there
Underground to Bank Station (District & Circle Line). Walk down Prince's Street to Gresham Street. Turn left then right into Basinghall Street. The Guild is directly opposite the Guild Hall.

The Guild is an example of the way pubs are changing to cater to a new market. Closer links with Europe have brought a preference for wine instead of beer. The Guild has a beer bar on the ground floor but the food and wine bar are combined downstairs.

While the beer bar is contained in a small area, the larger area below ground is more important. Down below the place is decorated partly in the English tradition (old oak casks are scattered about the floor, alcoves are panelled in dark oak with prints on the walls) and partly in the French style (the staff is French). The supporting columns are arranged in arches and are painted in a light colour and are lit to give a bright effect. The general effect is of a discreet place. The French influence leads to imaginative cuisine. On the menu appears octopus, which has of necessity to be cooked perfectly. There is also smoked salmon with mayonnaise served in a half avocado. The wines are extensive and sophisticated.

The people who come here obviously buy their suits in Savile Row rather than in Oxford Street, and the 'rounds' are in terms of bottles of wine rather than pints of beer.

The Guild takes its name from the Guild Hall, directly across the street. Here the aldermen conduct the affairs of the City of London. One of their number is elected to be Lord Mayor of London who governs the square mile of the City of London. He is not to be confused with the Mayor of Greater London, who controls the destinies of the well over four-hundred square miles of Greater London. The power of the Lord Mayor of London is expressed by the fact that the Queen has to obtain permission from him in order to enter the City of London. But while the Lord Mayor of London is appointed by the Guilds, the Mayor of Greater London is merely a politician.

The Lord Mayor of London has his own police force and his own regiment called the Honourable Artillery Company. Tradition is obviously more potent than the democratic process in the City of London. Nevertheless, London is changing. The Guild is not traditional. It has been designed to cater for the changing tastes of City men, who nowadays seem to prefer a continental lunch to the old 'pie and a pint'.

MARKET PUBS

From a visitor's point of view, at a market one can not only browse to admire, but can buy and take home that which one admires.

Islington's Camden market sells antiques. Browsing along the narrow Camden Passage which is lined with art galleries and antique shops, there is always the hope that one will find that beautifully decorated snuff box; a cut glass decanter, a small painting in oils.

The market at Petticoat Lane is a different kettle of fish. Pushing through the crowds in the streets of this market in Whitechapel, one is not so much impressed with the merchandise but the holiday spirit which always seems to linger there – even if a police car broadcasts a message from the Bishopsgate end of 'The Lane' that there are pickpockets about. There is a tradition that at Petticoat Lane one can have a watch stolen at one end of The Lane and buy it back (at the Pickpocket Arms) at the other.

Petticoat Lane is really a series of interconnecting streets which run from Bishopsgate Street in the City, to Commercial Road in the East End – roughly a mile. In the market they sell petticoats by the bale or individually. They sell reach-me-down suits, china, parrots, jewellery and jellied eels one eats from a basin standing up. At Monicadams 'caff' they sell good coffee and a cook brings up a tray of freshly baked pastries at what seems like quarter hour intervals. A Cockney Lady with weather-beaten skin and hands like fish-hooks, will lift pickled herring out of a barrel for your consumption – with masses of onion she shreds like lace in front of your eyes. A Pakistani, looking professionally mysterious, will tell your fortune and send you away clutching a packet of incense. A man selling candy will bamboozle you with his histrionics and confide in you that his wares are so cheap because they 'fell off the back of a lorry'. There is a man – always on a bicycle – who comes from Brittany in France, selling strings of onions which he wears round his neck like garlands and a Jewish jeweller similarly festooned – but with strings of pearls.

Petticoat Lane is the last bastion of Cockneys before they disappear altogether into a more sedate world of formal education and respectability – or they are levelled out into the standard citizen by the 'telly' and credit cards.

Petticoat Lane is traditionally Jewish and does not open on the Jewish sabbath. It opens on a Sunday but Jews are hardly a majority: there are Arabs, Turks, Hindus, Pakistanis, Cypriots, West Indians and variations of all these amongst the vendors. Mainly they speak Cockney as a *lingua franka*.

The pubs in a market are always crowded with a motley throng – as much on the spree as shopping. If there is a piano in the pub, a sing-song is always liable to occur.

Covent Garden, the most famous market of them all, has not been included in this section since it is no longer a market but a way of life – see the section on Covent Garden.

THE NEWMARKET
West Smithfield, EC1

How to get there
Underground to Farringdon or Number 17 bus from London Bridge to Smithfield Market.

The Newmarket faces the long, drawn out facade of the market from across the street. You will recognize it by the hand barrow smothered by geraniums and ivy which creep out of the barrow it is planted in, to blanket the facade of the building, giving it a rural look.

The pub, at least its public bar, is a meat-porter's pub, made for drinking the out-of-fashion beers – such as draft Bass and Worthington and good solid grub.

I decided to eat there when I caught the aroma from a steaming dish of salt-beef that the landlord had just brought up from the kitchen. The beef was delicious and of meat-porter proportions. When it was ready, a barman with a busted nose and cauliflower ear, provided service by the simple expedient of shouting "oo gets the salt beef?" I knew better than to offer him a tip.

A group of porters with their 'perks' of beef or pork wrapped in plastic lying at their feet – it would have been a plaited straw bag years ago – sat round a deal table drinking rounds of draft Bass. One of the party proffered an empty glass to his mate and in a sly Cockney way intimated that it was his turn to buy a round of drinks, by holding up his glass and innocently inquiring, 'think that will hold a pint, Mate?'

Behind the bar there is a black and white print of the old Smithfield Market, showing flocks of sheep penned in a large area on the field that was to become Smithfield. In those days, a butcher would buy a flock of sheep, cut their throats there and then and butcher them before packing them in his wagon. Nowadays the meat arrives in huge refrigerated lorries, thus eliminating the 'gutters running with blood' of the old days.

London is flooded with oceans of 'real-ale' from breweries in Yorkshire or the Midlands, but in this pub, they do not go with the tide. They continue to drink Bass or Worthington which requires skilled handling to keep in condition.

If you can indulge in the gruesome task of drinking beer at 6am, this is the place where – with the indulgence of the magistrate – it happens, since this is the time that the meat porter takes his breakfast. There is a downstairs bar packed at lunchtime with office types, mostly from legal firms in the vicinity. The two bars could not be more separate than if one was in Timbuktu.

THE LAMB TAVERN
Leadenhall Market, EC3

How to get there
By Underground (District & Circle Line) to Monument. Just around the corner from the station is the historical monument to the Great Fire of London which started and also finished here. Leaving this at your back, walk down Gracechurch Street past Fenchurch Street – on your right is the entrance to the market. The Lamb is inside the market. Looming over it is the building which houses Lloyds of London.

The Lamb sits on a formidable piece of real estate since it is the site of the Great Basilica (The Roman Forum) of the city the Romans called Londinium. Just down the road at the junction of Leadenhall and Gracechurch Streets a monument called London Stone marks the junction of Roman roads from north and east.

When Leadenhall Market was established, humping poultry being a thirst inducing activity which had to be assuaged, the Lamb was established on the spot. Only the best beer would do for the porters and it is so today – Young, Bass and Wetherall being the favoured breweries. It is the sort of place where, in the event of a customer holding up his glass to examine it against the light, the Publican will instruct the cellarman to change the barrel, which indicates that the men from Lloyd's who frequent the bar nowadays are as fussy about their beer as the porters were.

In such an historical locality there are bound to be a few legends and one of them concerns a character nicknamed Mother Goose who sold her geese in the market. She came from a farm in the country and drove the gaggle of geese before her. Worried about the sufferings of her charges, whose feet became sore through walking on the rough roads, her maternal instincts moved her to devise straps of leather to protect them. Henceforth the porters of the market nicknamed her Mother Goose. In case you may believe this to be a fairy story, take the trouble to cut through to Hart Street which is only a few minutes walk away in the direction of Tower Hill. There you will find a church called Saint Olive's where Pepys was once a churchwarden. You will find that Mother Goose is buried in the churchyard.

The porters of the market had to wait until 1780 until they could quench their thirst in the Lamb but they continued to do so for the next 200 years. It was rebuilt in 1881. At the time of writing, it is being reconstructed internally, but not exclusively as a porters' pub. The original 19th century structure with it's glass roofed arcades – supported by slim pillars topped by the City of London dragon picked out in silver and red – has not been disturbed. The Lamb, will continue to survive, in the manner of pubs, by recreating itself over and over to meet the demands of customers.

A detail from the etched glass in the Camden Head.

The market lies within the City of London from whence all except workaholics have departed by 6pm. In consequence, it closes its doors by 7.15pm and keeps them closed on Saturdays and Sundays.

CAMDEN HEAD
2 Camden Walk, Islington, N1

How to get there
Underground (Northern line) to Angel station. From the station, turn right into Islington High Street. Continue down Camden Passage to Camden Walk.

The pub is a genuine relic from Victorian London. It has beautifully etched glass panels in both doors and windows. Mahogany and oak panelling inside make it a candidate for exhibition in the antiques market in which it stands. There is a beer garden outside which is lighted by globes at night gives the impression of duplicate moons lingering in the branches. In the narrow alleys of the market, art galleries jostle antique shops. The ten minutes it should take to walk the length of Islington High Street to Camden Walk is liable to take an hour if you are into antiques. The pub derives it's name from William Camden who was an antiquary.

The Camden Head is a theatre pub which produces shows on Friday and Saturday at 8.30pm – usually comedy – performed by a company called Meccano.

The beer is good – particularly IPA, but Youngers and Newcastle Ales are also good. Food is ordinary but there is a famous fish and chip shop a couple of minutes away farther north on Upper Street where they have no licence to sell alcohol, but don't mind you taking in a drink – and if you have to wait for a table, Olga the Major Domo will feed you some chips (French fries) to stave off the pangs of hunger. You'll enjoy the cosmopolitan company since it's fame has spread to at least, America and Australia – in fact anywhere that English is the mother tongue. If your gastronomic juices are not stirred by fish and chips, the Camden does lunches on normal week days.

NOSTALGIC PUBS

Certain pubs in London invoke a feeling of nostalgia in a Londoner. The Old Bull & Bush is one of these. In former days, a blue collar worker had little to spend on holidays, and preferred to spend what he had on one or two good days at Easter or August Bank Holiday at the giant fair that was held on Hampstead Heath.

Cockneys are a fast disappearing breed and your modern Londoner is more likely to save his money for a couple of weeks in Majorca or Corfu. But the name Old Bull & Bush still arouses a feeling of nostalgia for the 'good old days' even though they were largely illusionary, perhaps not even particularly happy – a fact that the mind glosses over.

The so-called French Pub – it's real name is the York Minster – arouses memories of World War II because it was the unofficial headquarters of the Free French who had escaped across the English Channel to fight alongside the British. The Free French leader was General De Gaulle who took as his emblem the Cross of Lorraine. De Gaulle was a proud man – bitter in defeat and quick to uphold the rights of France. Of him, Winston Churchill commented that "of all the crosses he had to bear, the Cross of Lorraine was the heaviest!"

However, the 'crowded hour of glory' for the French pub has long since passed and the people who made it something special have gone too. On reassessment it appears to be just an ordinary little pub in Soho which has nothing to recommend it any more.

OLD BULL & BUSH
North End Way, Hampstead, NW3

How to get there
Underground to Hampstead Station (Northern line), then N⁰. 268 bus to Bull & Bush.

Come! come! come and make eyes at me
Down at the Old Bull & Bush.
Come! come! come and tell lies to me
Down at the Old Bull & Bush...

So sang the famous Music Hall singer, Florrie Ford; endearing herself to her Cockney audience and immortalising the Old Bull & Bush pub.

Florrie Ford was capitalising on the popularity of the pub as much as lending it her patronage, for it had already become an institution – the place to go after the coconut shies, the Ferris Wheel, the Cakewalk and all the other terrifyingly delicious thrills of the giant fair (Carnival) that sprawled over the hills and dales of Hampstead Heath at Easter and August.

At the Bull & Bush, Mum could rest her feet and sip her Port and Lemon and Dad could buy pints of beer to wash down the dust kicked up by the thousands of feet trampling the heath; the kids could be dispatched with an ice cream to chase through the bowers of the large garden shaded by yews, which unfortunately has had a large bite taken out of it to provide a car park.

Later, in the old public bar, which has been christened The Florrie Ford Bar, they would, for sentimental reasons, sing her song. Certainly they would dance to the tune of 'Knees Up Mother Brown' which is calculated to get even Grandma on her feet.

The old Saloon bar is posher, it is now called The William Hogarth Bar, after the satirist of the 18th century, whose house once stood here. Although he would have found more scope for his pencil in the Public Bar.

The discerning have always sought out the salubrious air of Hampstead with it's rolling woodlands and country air so conveniently close to town. Many of the famous have chosen it: Charles Lamb, Pitt, Reynolds, Garrick, Gainsborough, all strolled across the heath. Down by the Leg of Mutton Pond, there is a spot called The Vale of Health for obvious reasons. The Heath is high above London's stale air and, at times, fogs so thick one could hardly see across the road. What better incentive to pay a visit to The Old Bull & Bush.

RECLUSIVE PUBS

Reclusive pubs are not so because they choose to be. Obviously, the better they are known, the better their trade. They become so because they are shut in by building developments – even though, in the case of the Cutty Sark the builder was as august as the Royal Naval College.

Greenwich was once a small village on the river before the Royals took it up and built a palace there where Henry the Eighth was born and held three of his marriages. It is also the place where the Royal Observatory established the prime meridian (zero longitude) and it is possible for the tourist to stand on a line drawn on the ground with one foot in the western longitude and one in the east.

William and Mary, who never seemed to have acted singly, commissioned Sir Christopher Wren to build a hospital for sailors there. Wren could never do anything on a small scale and the building he had built was so magnificent that it was found to be much too good for common sailors and became the Royal Naval College instead.

THE CUTTY SARK
Ballast Quay, Greenwich, SE10

How to get there
From Westminster Pier at the foot of Big Ben, take a boat to Greenwich pier where there are lots of beautiful and fascinating things to see – like the elegant house built for the Queen by Inigo Jones and the imposing Royal Naval College, designed by Christopher Wren which is close to the pier. To get to the Cutty Sark pub start from the pier and follow a footpath by the river which traverses the facade of the Royal Naval College building. Make a jink to the right and almost immediately to the left past the Trafalgar Inn and continue down a narrow alleyway that passes Trinity Hospital – now an almshouse – to Ballast Quay which is only half it's name because it refers only to the river side of

the quay. On the landward side of the pub, according to the landlord, it is called Union Street. There you will find the Cutty Sark pub.

Half the fun of visiting the pub is getting there. Along the way you get an impression of Greenwich as it was centuries ago.

If you are in a car you can get directly to the pub from the main road but you will miss the best view of the college, which Wren obviously intended to be viewed from the river. You will also miss Trinity Hospital whose only means of access is by way of narrow alleyways that lead past the backs of the pubs. Only the frontage was important and no doubt the builders jostled each other to be on the water – squeezing into every foot of available space – leaving only pedestrian ways behind. When the Watermen plied their trade on the river it would be most convenient to drop off the passengers at a pub.

While the mighty made much of Greenwich – there is a Royal palace there where Henry VIII was born and later perpetrated three of his marriages. William and Mary, who never seem to have done anything alone, invited Sir Christopher Wren to design a hospital for seamen which turned out to be much too good for the likes of common seamen and became the Royal Naval College – there is actually a seaman's hospital in a tiny corner of the property.

One aspect of the changes brought about by the Second World War can be seen in the pubs of Greenwich which have woken up to the fact that they too are a part of history. The Cutty Sark, has come a long way from serving pints of beer to corduroy trousered labourers fresh from shovelling ballast on the quay. The owners renovated it's Georgian facade and a very fine staircase inside that leads up to a good restaurant where for high days and holidays you can order a whitebait dinner which is a British tradition too. It serves real-ale pulled up from the cellar by pumps on the fine bar; but you may prefer to sit outside with a view of the ancient river Thames. They cherish ancient traditions and have even been known to stage Morris Dancing there!

EXCLUSIVE PUBS

Exclusive pubs do not so much want to exclude as to include the best type of people by providing an atmosphere of refinement. Usually located in a posh neighbourhood, their outward appearance is attractive. Their inward appearance is rather like that of an exclusive club frequented by the upper crust of society where the food is of the best – there is usually a restaurant with a French chef. They are reclusive too – with the exception of El Vino's – which is in Fleet Street. They are the kind of pub that someone knows of and takes you there because it is his favourite pub. They do not offer any form of amusement – conversation has to suffice. Curiously, they are 'locals' where neighbours or members of a common profession foregather.

EL VINO'S
47 Fleet Street, EC4

How to get there
Underground to Temple Station. Walk up through The Temple to Fleet Street. The Temple station is closed on Sunday but so is El Vino's. The pub also closes early on Saturday evening.

Do not enter tieless or you will be told gently, almost apologetically, "You have to wear a tie, Sir". This place is a haunt for legal eagles from the adjacent Temple where they have their chambers – not offices. Their fees are in guineas – not pounds. On the job they wear a uniform which is out of date by centuries. Obviously, any pub they favour has to conform to their standards. If you can afford a Savile Row suit to set off the tie, so much the better. The barman – I almost wrote butler – will then enquire after your health. Amongst the clever, confident faces of the regulars there used to be more top flight journalists. Since Fleet Street went to Wapping there are fewer, but the wine list is still as long as your arm. They still serve ten varieties of champagne and the sandwiches are still served with cress. The discreet alcoves hold small parties of men who give the impression that they have important activities awaiting them 'in Chambers'. It may be pure coincidence that women are not exactly encouraged – in typical legal form by an ordinance that did not allow them to buy a drink at the bar – but recently, with the advent of more lady barristers, the rule had to be relaxed. Having won the victory, women do not appear to avail themselves of the prize of buying their own drinks however. The place is much a preserve where men can feel uninhibited by the presence of women. Not that there is the slightest sign of impropriety, but characters tend to blossom – wear double breasted waistcoats, sport a monocle, wear red striped shirts with a white collar, or indulge in such out of date customs as tying a linen napkin round the neck when dining. It goes with the atmosphere.

El Vino's is a place best observed at lunch time or before say 7pm. After then, it becomes very quiet since the interesting characters have gone home. It is one of those places where far more wine is sold than beer.

THE GRENADIER
18 Wilton Row, SW1.

How to get there
Underground (Piccadilly line) to Hyde Park Corner. From the exit on the south side of Hyde Park Corner, walk westward along Knightsbridge to Old Barrack Road which will be on your left. Follow this through to Wilton Row.

You have but to see the military sentry box outside the front door to realise that this is a pub steeped in military tradition. There was a military barrack here once and what then was the officer's mess of The Duke of Wellington's regiment is now The Grenadier, indeed, The Duke stabled his horse in the cobble-stoned yard and the mounting-block is still there. From here, in 1815, the Grenadiers marched off to Waterloo to defeat Napoleon.

The Grenadier is a pretty little pub with a grape vine trailing across it's front and the horseblock – now steps.

The Grenadier.

·LONDON PUBS

The pub lies in the London's 'poshest' area. Buckingham Palace is a few minutes walk away and Apsley House, where The Duke of Wellington lived, is as close. It has the intimate atmosphere of a local; maybe because it is hidden away in an obscure cobble-stoned yard approached through a narrow alley, known only to locals. The end of the yard in which it is situated, ends in an imposing arch which doesn't go anywhere. It once marked the entrance to the stables of the old barracks. The yard is lined by tiny houses, once occupied by NCOs of the regiment but now expensive flats with an excellent address. As one would expect of the locality, the clientele are not blue-collar workers.

The Grenadier has a ghost, a mournful one who was once an officer of the regiment. The story goes that he was caught cheating at cards and was flogged unmercifully by his peers; so brutally, in fact, that he died. Now he returns in spirit presumable to complain that manslaughter was rather overdoing the punishment for a misdemeanour.

The pub has the sort of bric-a-brac that landlords offer as evidence of past events, but the fact remains that history is on his side; the guards did march off from here to Waterloo; the great duke did frequent the place which salutes a military prowess unlikely to be seen in the foreseeable future.

A Mr Tattersall started a horse trading business in the mews which grew into the legendary Tattersall's of British horse racing fame.

THE RED LION
Waverton Street, W1.

How to get there
Underground to Hyde Park Corner (Piccadilly line) taxi from station.

The Red Lion is a pretty little pub enclosed in a corner where Waverton Street makes a right angled bend. There is sitting room outside on a portico masked by hanging baskets of flowers.

This is Mayfair – a posh area where few people are rich enough to live.

Inside the pub, two stockbrokers; one smiling and sharply decisive the other hesitant and indecisive, discuss a Stock Exchange transaction. It was not difficult to decide which of the two locals had had a good day.

Although the furniture of the bar had been arranged to provide intimacy here and there, the type of person who calls it a local prefers to stand with legs astride in the middle of the bar floor conversing with his intimates as though he were at home or in a gentleman's club – which, with its dark oak panelling hung with discreetly lighted prints, the place resembles. Suave and softly spoken, the staff who are either French or Spanish add to this effect.

The pub has a restaurant – more important than the bar – which serves elaborate and expensive meals.

The Saville Row dressed locals, are not the only people who use the place; at around five thirty people – also well dressed – from service industries also drop in for a quick one before going home.

YE OLDE MITRE TAVERN
Ely Court, Ely Place, EC4

How to get there
Underground (Central line) to Chancery Lane. From station, walk east down Holborn Viaduct past Hatton Garden – the international diamond centre – to the next turning on the left -Ely Place.

Finding Ye Olde Mitre is rather like tracing your ancestry – you have to work at it. First you enter the cul-de-sac called Ely Place which is named after the Bishops of Ely in Cambridgeshire who owned the land and had a town house built here in the 13th century, then you look for the sign of Ye Mitre, but a casual glance will reveal only the windows of law offices in this placid backwater off the torrent of Holborn. A more searching look will yield a tiny alleyway blocked by two iron bars which will allow you – if you are not too wide – to traverse the alley to it's end where you will find Ye Olde Mitre, appropriately under the sign of a bishop's mitre.

Ely Place is a private road and does not qualify for the protection of the City of London Police, instead it has an official Beadle who closes the gate each night, which signifies closing time for the pub too. No doubt the bars narrowing the alleyway were the idea of some long-forgotten Beadle.

The Bishops built their palace in the 13th century but the pub, which was supposed to have been for the use of the servants, was not built until 1547. Naturally it has been rebuilt over the centuries. The existing building it quite small and the tiny rooms have been kept partitioned in the original manner which enhances their coziness.

The customers are quiet well-mannered gents – mainly young – and probably from the law offices in Ely Place; they may be perceived in earnest contention in the tiny beer garden. There is a sense of continuity about the place – a sense of all the lawyers who ever came here over the centuries. In the 16th century, Sir Christopher Hatton leased most of the Bishop's land for a rent of one red rose, ten loads of hay and ten pounds sterling, annually ... but then, the handsome and dashing Sir Christopher was a great favourite of Queen Elizabeth I. He is said to have danced round a cherry tree with her, the tree is still in existence there.

It is significant that pubs have become respectable – although, for some reason, brewing has always been so. Pubs often receive the official accolade of being recognised as landmarks. The Mitre has been listed as an ancient monument; rebuilding cannot be undertaken with out the consent of a Government official. The term Ancient Monument may, to the visitor, seem to fit oddly on a building which has served the Public for years and continues to do so as a living entity, but at least 'The Establishment' has recognised it as being a part of London's history that refuses to die.

LITERARY PUBS

Historically, taverns have been the resort of poets and wits. Shakespeare was known to have engaged in drinking matches in his youth – the character of Sir John Falstaff could only have been created by a man who knew the bar-room type.

Writers like Ben Johnson, Beaumont, Fletcher and Donne would engage in contests of wit in such places as the Mermaid or The Devil's Tavern.

In the 18th century, Sir Richard Steele who frequented taverns with Addison wrote the famous letter to his wife in which he assured her that 'he would be with her within a half bottle of wine'. He and Addison not only garnered material for their essays in the *Spectator* and *Tatler*, but sometimes wrote them in taverns.

In the Cheshire Cheese, Dr Johnson presided over contests of wits with friends who included Goldsmith, Boswell, David Garrick and Sir Joshua Reynolds. Apparently the uninhibited atmosphere of a pub plus congenial company, stimulates rather than stultifies the literary ego.

THE COCK
22 Fleet Street, EC4

How to get there
From Charing Cross there are streams of buses along Fleet Street. Nos 6, 9, 11, 15, 83, 85, 86. The nearest Underground station is at Aldwych but it is only open at rush hours (going to work and coming home times). Get off the bus when you see the monument Temple Bar which is in the middle of the road just past the Law Courts. The Cock is opposite Temple Bar.

> 'Oh plump head waiter at the Cock
> To which I most resort,
> How goes the time? 'Tis five o'clock
> Go fetch a pint of Port.'

Thus wrote Tennyson where he not only drank the Port but enjoyed the food so much that he became a regular at the place.

Tennyson was not the only literary gent to patronise The Cock. Charles Dickens loved the place. One can imagine the handsome, ebullient Charles as the centre of a circle whose antecedents lay in the original Cock which was a direct descendant of the 17th century coffee houses where journalists resorted to pick up the latest news in much the same way as merchants dropped into Lloyd's coffee house to gain the latest news about cargoes. Each coffee house/tavern would attract those with common interests: St James for politics, Jonathan's for commerce and The Grecian for literature. All clustered around the Cock in those days.

Nowadays the stars that glitter at the Cock are legal luminaries since it backs on to the Temple which is not a place of worship – although the Knights Templars made it their headquarters and built a round Norman temple there which is still in an excellent state of preservation. The Knights Templars have long since disbanded and Barristers have established their Inns of Court there in an oasis of tranquil gardens and cobble-stoned courtyards walled off from the din of Fleet Street.

The atmosphere of calm continuity extends to the Cock where gentlemen in good suits discourse on the issues of the day – maybe a *cause celebre* being heard in the law courts across the street.

The original Cock can be traced back to Shakespeare's day. The present incumbent was rebuilt in 1882 but many of the internal fittings were retained – the 17th century chimney-piece, for example and the original sign which is said to have been carved by Grinling Gibbons. An elaborately carved wooden facade surrounds the downstairs bar contrasting with the London brick interior walls to give a soft, warm look.

That indefatigable man about town, Pepys, 'sang and made merry with Mrs Knipp, an actress, 'til almost midnight' here. It is unlikely that singing would be encouraged in the modern Cock but it is a rare place for a sandwich and a glass of wine after a stroll around the Temple or a visit to the Public Records Office in nearby Chancery Lane. Lunch is served on weekdays in the restaurant.

Temple Bar marks the division between The City of London and the City of Westminster. If you should happen to be looking out through the front window of the Cock at about 11.30am on the second Saturday of November you will see the Lord Mayor of London's annual procession pass by. He will be seated in a carriage every bit as pompous as the Monarch's. Once he is west of Temple Bar, however, he will be in the Monarch's Territory and he will stop his coach in order to descend to swear fealty to the Crown.

London is a city where stones hold stories and tradition never dies; only a hundred yards away the church of St Clement Danes splits the traffic of the Strand. From its bells issues the tune of the ancient nursery rhyme. 'Oranges and lemons'.

Back in the Cock the waiter is ready to serve you a pint of Port, as he did in Tennyson's day, except that he will not be there on weekends because the pub is closed.

THE MUSEUM TAVERN
49 Great Russell St, WC1

How to get there
Underground to Tottenham Court Road (Northern line & Central line). From the station walk north along Tottenham Court Road to the first turning on the right which is Great Russell Street. The Museum Tavern is about three hundred yards down on the right, opposite to the British Museum.

This is an intellectual pub. You'll find at least one bearded man with a domed brow in tense discussion with a companion whose fine hands make eloquent gestures of understanding or dissent. The pub has known the Bloomsbury set with such people as John Maynard Keynes expounding revolutionary theories about the world's economy with Virginia Wolfe making the eloquent gestures. In it's time the sought-after table in the corner would have crackled with the St Elmo's fire of Oscar Wilde's wit and when he had money – even Karl Marx – munching a cheese roll and sipping his pint before going back to the reading room of the British Museum across the street to resume his work on *Das Kapital* or the *Communist Manifesto*. Lenin too did research at the BM reading room and might well have used the tavern, but not for political meetings... it's single narrow bar is much too small.

Don't stay away from the place if you are not an intellectual... the food, both cold and hot, is really good. The pub is a 'free house' – that is free to sell any brewery's beer. It has a wonderful choice of real-ales and is the nearest place for resting feet tired from tramping the corridors of the museum. It has pleasant surroundings too, with a panelled ceiling supported by moulded figures and acid etched mirrors that would have had the late John Betjeman ooh!-ing and ah!-ing. It is an interesting pub – push open the door and you are met by the bustle and stir of people talking about things that interest or excite them. It sometimes gets overcrowded in the Tourist season - even then, it is a great pub. It's opening hours are 11.00am to 11.00pm.

COCKNEY PUBS

The definition of a Cockney is one 'born within the sound of Bow Bells' – meaning the sound of the bells of Bow church in the City of London at Cheapside. Nowadays this area is far from being a residential one, so few could qualify. A more modern definition might include those Londoners who speak with a Cockney accent – which swallows aspirates and scorns the glottal stop, so that Hampstead sounds like 'ampstid' and butter sounds like 'bu-er'; three become 'free' and a Cockney ornithologist will explain that that there are 'free fahsan fevvers on a frushes froat'. To tell a Londoner whose accent has become moulded by listening to the BBC, that he speaks with a Cockney accent is to insult him (notwithstanding that among his peers there are some who would hold him in scorn for trying to speak 'posh' like a BBC announcer).

A true Cockney likes to flavour his speech with words from the Hindi or Arabic. He indulges in 'rhyming slang' so that a Dollar becomes an Oxford Scholar or a suit a Whistle and Flute.

Bernard Shaw who was an Irishman, loved to mock the English class attitude towards their native tongue. His *Pygmalion* was a play about Cockney speech: in it a Cockney flower 'Gel' becomes a lady by changing her accent from the gorblimey to the sublime-y. Centuries ago a Cockney Gel – Nell Gwyn – became the mistress of a king and founded an aristocratic dynasty. Apart from her beauty she was witty and good natured – a prototype Cockney.

Years ago a Cockney would blow his wages on one glorious binge over a weekend then pawn his best suit on Monday – nowadays he uses a credit card to take a 'Bird' to a 'posh' place for dinner. He leaves school at a later age than his father did and prefers to work in the City where his quick wits bring him large bonuses. Through exposure to the BBC he may have forced his vocal chords to use the glottal stop and to explode a few aspirates in his sentences, but he will still refer to criticism as a 'diabolical liberty'.

Most Cockney pubs are in the 'East End' (the area around the docks of the Port of London) or 'over the other side' (meaning south of the Thames – more particularly south-east).

THE FOX & FIRKIN
316 Lewisham High Street.

How to get there
British Rail from London Bridge to Lewisham station. From station turn left to junction with High Street then turn right into High Street. The Fox and Firkin is 10 minutes walk away down High Street on the left hand side. Alternatively bus No. 36 or 36a from Victoria. By car take A20 to Lewisham.

This is a real Cockney pub where the locals come to blast out songs – from a song sheet obligingly provided – to the tune of a piano. There is a pulpit dominating the large bar which becomes part of the festivities. Nobody knows from which church it came, but it is in line with the Bruce Brewery Company's sense of humour – and encourages the curious to come – if only to check it out.

The Underground system has largely ignored South London in favour of the above-ground rail system which is also electrified but does not have the profusion of stations provided by the Underground system. Bus journeys take longer because of traffic problems, hence South London tends to be isolated from the influx of newcomers that ameliorated North London – in the traffic sense - hence the last vestiges of Cockneys are more likely to be found in South London – certainly in the Fox & Firkin which is a rollicking pub with music played every night. The singing is aided and abetted by the real-ales brewed on the premises. Their names are Porter, Bitter, and Dogbiter. One can see these being brewed by squinting through the observation panels provided by the matey management.

On a Friday or Saturday night this is a great 'boy meets girl' pub with a bucolic atmosphere that makes introductions unnecessary. The festivities begin with the music which starts at 9.00pm every evening.

GOOSE & FIRKIN
47 Borough Road, SE1

How to get there
Underground to Elephant & Castle (Northern & Bakerloo lines). From Station walk north on Newington Causeway to Borough Road. The pub is five minutes walk down Borough Road on the right.

In case you are wondering, a firkin is a cask which holds 9 gallons of beer.

The Firkin Pubs are all owned by Bruce's Brewery which produces real-ales with names like Stoat, Ferret, and Dogbolter. These, along with others – according to the choice of the individual landlord – are brewed on the pub's premises. The Goose & Firkin brews Goose, Borough, Dogbolter and a liquid dynamite known as Gobstopper.

Situated opposite to a college of London University, the pub had to satisfy the appetites of youth. With the beer they serve Baps – a flat bread roll the size of a dessert plate which is sliced through the middle and filled with whatever the landlord makes available. They also serve the usual hot pub lunch.

The Goose & Firkin is filled, at lunchtime, with college students who are not interested in fine wines – or fine food – for pecuniary reasons. What they are interested in is eating, drinking and talking, in that order. On festive occasions they sing – an obliging landlord provides a piano.

You will not find Aubusson carpets or cut flowers – rather, wooden floors and sturdy tables and benches to take the weight of you bap, but the beer is freshly brewed and atones for all – particularly the self-service.

At lunchtimes even the standing room is only just adequate, but the atmosphere is unrestrained and charged with vigorous laughter and argument. The action is mainly at lunchtime when the Goose & Firkin is a noisy but bright and cheerful pub.

At weekends when the local residents come in, a 'sing-song' may well start. Being close to the area called The Elephant & Castle, in the past it was a Cockney area, but in this restless age the pubs customers may be a Polyglot crowd – even so the old Cockney ritual of dancing 'knees up Mother Brown' might occur – it depends upon how many Gobstoppers they have had.

THE COACH & HORSES
13 The Market, Greenwich SE10

How to get there
British Rail from Charing Cross to Greenwich then walk down Greenwich High Road past Greenwich Church following posted directions to the Cutty Sark (the famous old sailing ship). Just before the Cutty Sark there is an entrance to the Greenwich Market on the right. The Coach & Horses is in the market.

A better but slower way is from Westminster by boat to Greenwich Pier. From the Pier walk (2 minutes) in the direction of the main road to a market entrance on your right.

A pub used by the Cockney market porters for centuries, when the market became moribund it took to flirting with tourists and there are signs that it may become a second Convent Garden; nevertheless in spite of the bright umbrellas outside that give it a Continental air, it still retains it's Cockney identity. In the summer, the lunch trade is indubitably cosmopolitan but they still serve you mustard pickles with your Ploughman's lunch, the ale is good and they serve draft cider. In their cheeky Cockney way, they set the tables out on the market square. A poster invites you to a 'knees-up' (dance) on Thursday and you are invited to 'bring yer barrer but park it on the square'.

The setting is as authentic as Wren's Royal Naval College next door or Inigo Jones' Queen's House up on the hill.

On the north side of the pub there is a narrow alley which frames a view of the beautiful Cutty Sark now reposing in dry dock after it's exploits in the China Tea Trade. Francis

Chichester's Gypsy Moth – in which he single handed
sailed round the world – is there too, sitting modestly in
the last dock it will ever occupy. "That's nothing," says
the landlord, "when they set the meridian up at Greenwich
Observatory they set it to pass through the saloon bar of the
Coach and Horses."

The monster trucks under the mark of the EEC, snort
and roar along Greenwich High Road on their way to or
from Europe, but inside the Market Square the customers
of the Coach and Horses are cocooned in a time before the
snorting monsters invaded old London.

THOMAS A BECKET
Old Kent Road, Walworth, SE 17.

How to get there
No 53 bus from Westminster, going south via Elephant &
Castle. Ask bus Conductor to put you off at the Thomas A
Becket pub in The Old Kent Road.

If not as celebrated as The Tabard Inn of Chaucer's
Canterbury Tales, the Thomas A Becket was also a lodging
place for pilgrims to Canterbury, as a plaque on the side of
the building testifies. Do not anticipate any ecclesiastical
elegance. It is now a pugilists pub where boxers train in
a gym over the bar. The pub has been rebuilt over and
over and now shows no sign – apart from the plaque –
of the original hostel that sheltered pilgrims. If you follow
the manly art, you'll find it most interesting; if you do not,
it shows another facet of London's life that has no parallel.

For some of the important bouts that take place uptown –
say at the venerable Albert Hall – the weighing-in ceremony
often takes place here in the bar.

A miniature boxing ring is constructed on a stage with
the weighing in scales set in the middle of the ring. The
high priest of the ceremony – a slim bearded man with an
unctuous manner more suited to a funeral parlour – waves
a slim white hand to the only pugilistic looking man in a
group standing at the bar who puts his head back and in
purest Cockney, shouts "Nah! Smiff, lets 'ave yer." and

"ah!" He peers, under battle scarred eyebrows, at a slip of paper in his hand, "Dongola!"

Two young boxers – second generation West Indians now *bona fide* Englishmen – with skin that, under the powerful lights, has the light absorbing quality of soot, look up with wild African eyes. One of them corrects the trainer, "Dugonda!" he snaps, before ducking under the ropes of the mock ring.

The official makes meticulous adjustments and relays the information to the Trainer who shouts "Smiff made the weight at nine stone six".

Others follow; a blonde Scandinavian type who is technically American, chews gum fiercely as a means of distracting his thoughts from this alien place where officials look like undertakers. His manager, roly poly in the middle, pushes up to the bar and demands a grapefruit drink for his ' Kid' who parks his gum and drains the drink and holds his glass up for a refill. He only just made the weight.

"Are you nervous?" someone asks.

"I'm the nervous one" says his Manager, heroically accepting the role.

In spite of the atmosphere – boxing gloves used in championship bouts hang on he wall along with Henry Cooper's boxing boots and a Lonsdale belt – the boxers are not the 'Main Event'. This comes from the bulky businessmen in Saville Row suits, who confer gravely then smack hands at the consummation of a deal. One of them takes a sandwich proffered to him. He opens it and throws it down.

"Bloody smoked salmon again," he complains.

"Sorry!" says the Landlord, "We are out of caviar."

A group of Dutchmen establish themselves at a table. One of them – he has long, carefully trimmed blonde hair and a small moustache – sits looking sulky because nobody is taking notice of him. His manager goes off to beat the bushes for journalists.

He comes back with a man with a bald head who greets the boxer with "Remember me? I was the referee when you fought Davies".

The Dutch boxer, visibly relieved at being recognised, smiles: "Yah! yah! I recognise." He smacks the referee on the back.

"You working tonight?" the referee asks – meaning is he fighting.

"Och! nay. Today I drink and watch."

Today upstairs in the gym there is no activity. I come down to examine the mementos of Henry Cooper – a native son who trained here. When he fought Cassius Clay he put him on the canvas but over-eagerness cost him a narrow decision.

Boxing may be in the process of becoming respectable. Cooper is now a stockbroker... Clay became Mahommed Ali – a millionaire.

THEME PUBS

Theme pubs seek publicity by modelling their decor to suit a specific theme. The Sherlock Holmes at Charing Cross, adopts the master of deductive reasoning as it's patron saint and the decor in each bar is suited to the theme. They even have a reproduction of the great sleuth's study. It is not only for the seeming veracity of the portrayal alone, but because it is a handsome pub possessing solid comfort that it has been included in this book.

A theme must be interpreted very well if it is to charm the customers: intrigued by the theme, they will be disappointed if the facsimile fails to come up to their expectations – for example there is a pub which takes Jack the Ripper as its theme, but it merely displays a few newspaper clippings of the period and has a sign outside depicting a sinister figure. Other than that, this particular pub has nothing to recommend it. Another, which identifies itself with the London Fire Brigade in it's title, merely has its walls covered with a wallpaper that has fire-fighting as it's theme. Neither of these pubs has anything to offer in the way of comfort or charm ... which only goes to show the importance of *personal selection* ... the theme of this book.

SHERLOCK HOLMES
10 Northumberland Street WC2.

How to get there
Underground to Charing Cross (Northern & Bakerloo lines). Do not confuse the Underground station with that of the British Rail station which has an identical name. With your back to the Underground station, cross the thoroughfare of The Strand, turn left into The Strand (west), then Northumberland Street is the first turning on the right (one minute). Walk down Northumberland Street to its junction with Northumberland Avenue to the pub.

To take a walk down Northumberland Avenue is to walk back into the nineteenth century. Here is the site of the

Northumberland Hotel where Sir Henry Baskerville stayed (in *The Hound of the Baskervilles*) and had one of his new boots stolen. Here, opposite, set back into a recess with an old tree shading it's facade, is the Sherlock Holmes pub where you may have laid open for your inspection, the abode of literature's greatest sleuth.

Relics from his famous cases – even a cast of one of the great paws of a Baskerville hound – abound in the bars. Imaginatively, they have constructed his study upstairs. 'A clear case,' Holmes might have instructed Watson, 'of history imitating art'.

There are Sherlock Holmes Societies. What a ball they must have here! Around the corner, the Empire Society used to attract members from the far-flung corners of 'the Empire on which the sun never sets'. How ironic that the Empire is dead but Sherlock lives on! Certainly in this pub named after him.

The charade is carried out so well that one begins to have doubts. Was he really a figment of Conan Doyle's imagination? Who cares! Furnished impeccably it not only conjures up a Holmsian atmosphere but provides good food and drink in a cozy place that exemplifies the solid comfort of the best Victorian establishment and is so English that it may well be representing the theme of the best of English pubs. In the summer you may sit under the shade of the tree in front of the pub in an atmosphere that conjures up the clop of hooves rather than the roar of engines that is the bane of the Twentieth century.

DIRTY DICK'S
202 Bishopsgate, EC2.

How to get there
Underground to Liverpool Street (Circle and Metropolitan lines). Buses 5, 6, 8, 22, 25, 47, 78. The pub lies across the street from the Bishopsgate exit from Liverpool Street station.

This is a pub that carries the legend of a blighted life. Nathaniel Bentley, who later became known as Dirty Dick, was a real person. Left a fortune by his father, he became a man-about- town who wore the latest fashions; who had his hair done by a peruquier and dressed to kill. When he fell in love the whole world had to know. He busied himself in plans for a party to announce his engagement. There were visits to the tailor for him and the dressmaker for his intended. Caterers were called in to plan a sumptuous banquet. The party would be the greatest! He and his love would be the centre of attention.

Then disaster! On the eve of the party, his beloved was stricken fatally. In a moment she was dead.

Nathaniel never recovered from the blow; A completely self absorbed man, he decided that his life was finished. From being meticulous in all things, he swung to the complete opposite. He ordered the banquet room to be sealed; the feast left to the vermin. The Damask table cloth became soiled with rat droppings; the candelabra festooned with spider webs. Now he led a solitary life of bitterness and despair. He would not change his linen saying "it will only get dirty again". He became known as Dirty Dick.

Dirty Dick's pub perpetuates this legend. At one time the Vault Bar downstairs exhibited a show of stuffed bats. The owners allowed cobwebs to grow over the bar of Dirty Dick's.

Some relics are still exhibited in the vault, which is now mainly patronised by the young because there is rock and roll music played there.

The pub is owned by a wine house – they still bottle wine from wooden hogsheads in the vaults. The pubs specialities are port and sherry. The City office workers come to drink it and take bottles away with them. Upstairs there is an extensive snack bar which particularly prides itself on it's daily delivery of oysters from Whitstable.

The rules by which the house is governed are exhibited over the bar. They read:

'The shop being small, difficulty occasionally arises in supplying customers. We will be greatly obliged if you bear in mind the old axiom: when you are in a place of business, transact your business and go about your business.'

An injunction worthy of old Nat Bentley himself.

The pub keeps normal hours.

SURREY TAVERN
The Oval, Kennington, SE1

How to get there
Underground to Oval station on Northern line. Make a U turn left out of the station and the Surrey Tavern faces you.

If you are a cricketer you will appreciate that the Tavern actually tunnels – an ornate tunnel studded with bosses – into the ground under one of the stands. If you are not a cricketer, this is an excellent place to learn about cricket as you wander pint in hand amongst the gallery of press photos that bring back the dramatic moments of despair as stumps are smashed apart or joy at an open shouldered smash to the boundary during some bygone Test match when England played the likes of Australia or India or The West Indies. There is a large West Indian colony around here who bring their steel drums with them for the three days that it takes to play a match. At important matches the scene can resemble a religious revival, so virulent is the cricket bug when it takes. Naturally the pub carries it on T.V. for those who cannot get into the ground. There is not a lot of room in the tunnel-like bar on the ground floor, but there is ample space on the next floor up.

Outside of Britain (except for those far flung dominions of the late Empire) cricket is hardly known. The landlord exhibits notices which try to explain the game to those who were not brought up on it. It is a game which is played from 11 am to 6 pm for three consecutive days; where one side is 'in' but sits the game out in the pavilion except for two of it's team members while the side which is 'out' is playing in the field. It is, admittedly, a daunting task which the landlord tackles humorously. From his point of view, it is harvest time for three days, since people drop in for a couple of hours and then go back to work, throughout the three days. This arrangement keeps the beer moving and fresh and the sandwiches are fresh too.

The pub has the usual hours (11am to 11pm) and in summer time lunch is a movable feast. Summer time (late May until the middle of September) is the only time cricket is played in England. By the way – they stop the game to take tea each day at 4pm.

DOGGET'S COAT & BADGE
Blackfriars Bridge, SE1

How to get there
Underground to Blackfriars Station (Circle line). From station walk across to the south side of the bridge. The pub lies at the foot of the bridge.

From the front door of the pub you will be rewarded with a most impressive view of St Paul's Cathedral – particularly at night when the dome of the cathedral is silhouetted by flood lights. This alone can make your visit worthwhile, but further pleasure awaits inside, where the main bar has been rigged to make it resemble the 'tween decks space of a ship of Nelson's day.

The pub has been named for a boat race on the Thames; to quote the records of Watermans Hall for 1715: 'A race by six Watermen in the first year of their freedom...'

Actor Dogget prospered to become joint manager of Drury Lane Theatre. Being of a charitable nature he financed a race to be held annually with the winner to be rewarded with a coat and badge. What pecuniary reward went with the beautiful scarlet coat with a badge is large as a soup plate is not revealed but the coat and badge made him *ex officio* top Freeman on call for the Royal barge on state occasions.

Dogget died in 1721 and the authority for organising the race was bandied about, first being handled by the Admiralty Office, but later by the Warden of The Fismongers Company, who organised the race for a couple of centuries thereby making it one of the oldest continuing races in the world.

The race starts at the next bridge down stream from the pub and runs four miles and five furlongs to Chelsea. The significance of the course is that it was within the

Watermens' territory because, on the lower reaches of the river these were the only bridges; in between one had to hail a Waterman to be ferried across.

When the gentry interested themselves in rowing, large sums of money were wagered and no doubt the winner would be generously tipped by his backers. With the advent of engines the old type Waterman disappeared but the race is still held every year because tradition dies hard in England. The pub is not particularly a 'local' since the vicinity hasn't a large resident population. The customers tend to be young and lively in the evening and local businessmen at lunchtime. The pub keeps the usual opening and closing hours of 11.00am to 11.00pm. At lunchtime it provides pub lunches, hot or cold.

THE BLACKFRIAR
174 Queen Victoria Street, EC4

How to get there
Underground (District & Circle lines) to Blackfriars. The station deposits you outside the pub.

This pub has to be seen to be believed. Designed by an architect and a sculptor to express the theme of Art in Craft, every square inch of space is crammed with what, in the nineteenth century, was called Art Nouveau. Crammed into a tiny triangular space under a railway arch, the designers had to make every inch count. Walls, floors and even a bar has been sculptured from red, green and white marble. The ceiling of an inner bar has been formed by a series of arches adorned by multi-coloured mosaic including glittering gold.

In the 1950s, the pub was threatened by a traffic development but was saved by the plea that it stood on the site of a 13th century Dominican Priory. No trace of the priory remained but it gave the designers their theme – the life of the Brothers in the Priory.

The walls of the inner bar have been hung with hand beaten copper panels which show the life of the Brothers pursuing many activities including boozing. The panels are captioned by homilies which make salient points such as: 'A good thing is soon snatched away' and 'Don't advertise – tell a gossip'. There is a fishing scene captioned 'Tomorrow is Friday' and a gardening scene captioned 'Saturday afternoon'.

No square inch has been spared the craftsman's art and where a space was vacant between, say, black and white and beige marble columns, it has been filled in with mosaics or marble demons or angels or rabbits. Lights are held in wrought iron brackets. Bronze bas reliefs top mosaic and homilies are cut into the marble, for example – 'Wisdom is rare'. A massive open fireplace framed in marble and copper has inglenooks too. The effect is overwhelming.

The site of which the pub is only a small portion, is as historic as any in the City. It has seen the Romans who left a bit of their city wall. It has seen the Papal Court that refused Henry VIII a divorce from Catherine of Aragon and it has seen – just around the corner at the Blackfriar's Theatre – Shakespeare produce several of his plays. Here Charles I established the Royal Printing Works which printed the first copy of the King James Bible. In 1785 The Times was founded here in Printing House Square – later acquired by the present owner, Continental Illinois Corporation, in 1977.

Coming down to earth, the pub is a Free House selling Bass, Wetherhed and Charrington's beers. In spite of the so called Snack Bar, the Public Bar has the snacks. The hours are 11am to 10pm and the pub closes on Saturdays and Sundays.

THE LAMB
94 Conduit Court, WC1

How to get there
Underground to Russell Square (Victoria and Metropolitan lines). Turn left out of station towards Russell Square. Turn left at main road and walk along Southampton Row to Guildford Street (on left hand). Three minutes walk down Guildford Street brings you to Conduit Street on right. Conduit Court is off Lamb's Conduit Street.

The landlord has gone to great pains to recreate a Victorian atmosphere inside the pub – outside, the fabric of the building is much older. Look for a tiny alleyway by the side of the pub, to find, chiselled into the wall, an ancient notice which reads: 'This pump is erected for the use of the Publick'. Although smoothed and shallowed by the winds and rains of 200 years, the letters are still decipherable; obviously, the pump was made redundant by the introduction of public mains water. To a discerning eye such items may be unearthed round every corner in London – reflecting the ever changing modes of the Londoner's life.

Although the decor of the pub is determinedly Victorian, the separate bars have not been retained. Then, there would have been a separate bar called the Public Bar – mainly occupied by men, with the ladies ensconced in the Snug, with an elaborate carved screen of mahogany between them and the vulgar gaze. The attention of the barmaid could be attracted by opening a small swivelling window in the screen. The glass of the window was frosted to preserve anonymity. Other Victorian relics are everywhere. The walls are panelled in mahogany, the ceilings are planked, the mirrors and glass panels are bevelled and etched with elaborate sprigs and flourishes. The brass lamps are retained but now work by electricity.

The theme includes Victorian Theatre. On the walls, framed photographs of 'Artistes' of the Stage, looking elegant against backgrounds of aspidistras, or painted screens, gaze soulfully into space. Such stars as Marie Tempest, Charles Wyndham, Edna May, Elaine Terry and Hayden Coffin are there to recall an era when they were even more worshipped than modern film stars. A portrait of the beautiful Mrs Patrick Campbell recalls her interminable affair with George Bernhard Shaw, which was mainly conducted on paper.

On the counter is preserved a square, box-like instrument – it was the precursor to the gramophone – called the Polyphone. It has a large circular disc drilled with a number of holes and is inscribed romantically 'The Silver Slipper'. Give the barmaid twenty pence and she will return you a penny as big as a Maximilian dollar to put in the Polyphone which will shriek out a sentimental tune in a far away voice as remote as the beauties shown on the wall.

The customers of The Lamb are not locals. Some are attracted by the atmosphere and some by the excellent ale. The latter type is combative about the quality of the ale and are most likely to be members of a society that campaigns for 'real-ale' called CAMRA. They are mainly young and lively and, particularly at weekends crowd in to pursue their hobby.

The pub's hours are 11.00am to 11.00pm. There is a lunchtime trade but the main action is between 8.00pm and 11.00pm when people are attracted to this well-known pub to drink the good ale and talk the good talk. The atmosphere is friendliness personified.

PHOENIX & FIRKIN
Denmark Hill Railway Station, Windsor Walk. SE5

How to get there
185 bus from Victoria (adjacent to British Rail station in Vauxhall Road) or 176 bus from Charing Cross will put you off at the pub.

The Phoenix & Firkin is actually a British Rail station once called Denmark Hill, which expired and rose from the ashes to become a pub run by Bruce's brewery. It is a very handsome pub. The original building has been restored with pride and joy in the craftsmanship of unknown masons. The facade shows bosses that served no other function than to decorate. What the unknown mason was doing was to put his imprint on his work. Someone in the brewery too, has taken time and money to floodlight the facade to show off the brickwork. Inside, in what was once the booking hall, huge casts support the soaring ceiling. A gallery has been built up there with tables that look down on the people – mainly young – who crowd round the bar. The steps in front of the building are crowded with youngsters too, all amused by the idea of buying a pint where once people bought tickets.

Bruce's have obviously decided that what their pubs need is a gimmick to attract the crowd... then the crowd itself becomes an attraction.

Directly opposite the pub is the main entrance to the Salvation Army Training College. When he was alive, General Booth, the founder of the Salvation Army, thundered against 'The demon drink'. One wonders if his ghost hovers over the festivities across the way?

In accordance with their custom, The brewery makes the beer on the premises. The pub keeps the normal licensing hours of 11.00am to 11.00pm. The action is evening – particularly at weekends.

DRAG PUBS

Drag has always been accepted in the UK. In the heyday of Music Hall an actress called Vesta Tilley, had a very successful act in which she dressed like (a very pretty) young man, which gave her much scope to be dashing in a way that exhibited her femininity. The male 'drag queen' gets his effect by suddenly exhibiting his masculinity in some way. The outrageous contrast gets a laugh. He may be a moonlighting docker or truck driver who normally smokes a pipe. He is not necessarily 'gay' and a Drag pub is not necessarily one where Gays hang out. A Transvestite gets a thrill from wearing clothes of the other sex, but a public performer probably gets his kicks from arousing the audience.

THE NEW BLACK CAP
171 Camden High Street, NW, 1

How to get there:
Underground to Camden Town (Northern line). From station walk south (3 minutes) on Camden High Street. The pub is on the right.

The name Black Cap is a macabre reference to its former function as a courthouse. In the days when hanging was rife, it was the custom to place a square of black linen on the judge's head before he sentenced a convicted prisoner to death. The site of the court is now a pub where performances of drag – men made up to look like women – are given. Drag pubs flourish in the sort of neighbourhood that has a shifting population. They are usually furnished in the manner to which the customers are accustomed. The Black Cap is no exception. The drinking facilities are of the stand up kind either at the bar or in a long passage leading to the performance area. There is a good stage and plenty of standing room. The walls are lined with pictures of Drag Queens in their performance costumes.

Like the old time Music Hall artistes, the Drag Queens tour the circuit. Playing at Camden Town, Vauxhall, Elephant & Castle and Clapham. Their ripe, earthy humour with it's ribald defiance of convention is wickedly amusing. Naturally it attracts 'Gays' but by no means exclusively. There will be plenty of people there out of curiosity, particularly at weekends. One barman there has a novel way of identifying his customers preferences, while serving, he will put on an act of outrageous effeminacy meanwhile taking stock of the customer's reactions. If he decides that the customer is 'straight' the effeminate manner disappears and his screeching, mock Mayfair. accent disappears and reverts to it's normal Scouse (Liverpool) accent.

The Drag show is performed every night at 10-30pm and at lunchtime at weekends. While the drinks side of the festivities are adequate the cuisine is not a subject mentioned at the New Black Cap.

WINE CELLARS

Omar Khayam knew what he was talking about when he expressed a desire for 'A loaf of bread, a jug of wine and thou beside me' a phrase that should adorn every wine cellar because the candle-lit atmosphere they try to achieve invites the exchange of confidences that lead to intimacy ... which may be why women seem to prefer them. They sell wine by the glass, too.

GORDON'S WINE CELLAR
47 Villiers Street, WC2

How to get there
Underground (District line) to Embankment station. Exit the station on the north side to Villiers Street. Gordon's is about thirty yards up on your right, just past the entrance to a public garden called Watergate.

Watergate Garden houses the elegant stone arch that Inigo Jones designed to allow the barge of George Villiers, Duke of Buckingham, to pass through from York House to the river. It is one of Jones's less known works but not the least in elegance.

You will need to be alert to spot the entrance to Gordon's, since it does not go in for flashing lights or a top hatted doorman, instead look for a flight of stone steps that look as though they might lead to a cellar for that is what Gordon's is – a 300 year old cellar.

In the light of candles you will see bare brick walls covered only by the fungus that grows on them. in places water drips from the ceiling; one instinctively looks for bats that might possibly roost there – not that you will find them, of course.

Gordon's has a wine list that would bring a sparkle to the eye of Bacchus. The list is casually chalked up on a slate, but classified in a professional way; the Sherry is identified as, say, an Oloroso, or Amontillado, or Fino as are the Ports, the Burgundies, the clarets and the more esoteric Madeira and Malmsey.

The prices are for locals rather than tourists. The nearby Savoy Hotel wouldn't lose a moment of sleep over the competition where food is concerned, although sandwiches are cut to order, but Gordon's is a place to talk by candlelight over a bottle of good wine.

Gordon's is not subject to the usual licensing laws and may open and close as it pleases – another tale of an overspent King behind the granting of a favour to the Vintners Company by Edward III in the 14th century – the Vintners own Gordon's. In practice Gordon's opens at noon and closes at 9.00pm on weekdays and closes on Sundays. It is a very popular place particularly for the adventurous.

LOCALS

Locals – meaning pubs to which local residents regularly resort – are most likely to be found in a village. London really is a series of villages surrounded by miles of bricks and mortar. Some villages which have resisted the urban sprawl as in Dulwich Village where the land is owned by Dulwich College, have even managed to keep a rural atmosphere. Highgate is another example of a village in Greater London, but neither can be described as belonging to central London, even so, there are pubs in the centre of London that can be described as locals – mainly at lunchtime when regulars attend regularly because they work in the vicinity.

DOG & DUCK
18 Bateman Street, W1.

How to get there
Underground to Tottenham Court Road (Northern & Central lines). From station walk west on Oxford Street (3 minutes) to Soho Street which leads to Soho Square. Continue through square to Greek Street. Bateman Street is on left hand side.

Lying in the midst of the most sophisticated part of a sophisticated city, this homely little pub with its two small bars (the Saloon Bar has an open fire) looks as though it would be at home in the country not too far from a duck pond. It actually was in the 18th century when it was a place for tired duck hunters to rest by the fire. Somehow – in the heart of cosmopolitan Soho – the Dog & Duck has retained this ambience.

Soho takes it's name from a mansion built on the spot by The Duke of Monmouth, an illegitimate son of Charles II. Although his father bestowed the title on him, Monmouth wanted more – the throne. Later James contested this aspiration with the result that Monmouth was beheaded. Being, so to speak, without a head, the mansion that Monmouth built was acquired by Lord Bateman for whom Bateman street is named. At a much later date Bateman Street was to shelter a man who looked with contempt upon the idea that the acquisition of power and rank depended upon which bed a person happened to be born; the man was Karl Marx.

In his lighter moments Marx was fond of a drink and might have used The Dog & Duck as a local. Not for long, though ... because he was thrown out of his lodgings in Bateman Street for not paying the rent.

In 1926 in nearby Frith Street, an event occurred which was to have an effect on millions when John Logie Baird transmitted the first television picture.

The Dog & Duck is beyond the fringe for tour operators hence it is known only to the cognoscenti who cherish it for it's intimate atmosphere. It is as close as you will get to a local within the purlieus of Soho. The only type of amusement offered is conversation. This might be interesting since it's regulars number, a shoemaker who makes shoes for Royalty, a Scotland Yard man, a lady with a title who likes her pint and people from the world of film. It has a good snack bar. The pub keeps normal licensing hours.

THE OLD BELL
Fleet Street, EC4

How to get there
There are streams of buses that traverse Fleet Street Nos 6, 9, 11 and 15. Get off at The Daily Telegraph building. The Old Bell is on the south side of Fleet Street.

The great charm of London is the discovery of some oasis of timeless peace that has somehow continued to exist in the midst of the compulsive rush of modern life. The Old Bell is the gateway to such a discovery. While the front door opens onto the three ring circus of Fleet Street, the back door opens onto the cloistered calm of St Bride's Avenue – all of twelve feet away from St

Bride's churchyard (the width of St Bride's Avenue that is).

In the basement of St Bride's there are Roman ruins which you are invited to inspect and the remains of seven churches, one for each century of St Bride's history.

Samuel Pepys was born just around the corner in Salisbury Court – as a plaque on the Reuter building proclaims – and was baptised in the church.

From the pub's back door one looks straight on to the churchyard and the graves of Samuel Richardson, writer, also the grave of Caxton's pupil Wynkin de Worde, who, if he isn't the patron saint of journalists, ought to be since it was he who first brought printing to Fleet Street.

When Sir Christopher Wren rebuilt the church in 1675, he built what became The Old Bell as a shelter for his workmen. The typical Wren spire must have dominated the surrounding buildings; it still does except that it had to be rebuilt after an encounter with the Luftwaffe in 1940. Just around the corner in Salisbury Square, a weeping willow droops it's leaves over a memorial to some forgotten Lord Mayor, while pigeons coo from the trees in the churchyard. This, in the heart of a newspaper empire who sends it's minions rushing around the world seeking the news. Newspaper men have used the Old Bell for many generations. At lunchtime the single, U-shaped bar vibrates with their accounts of the latest from Vladivostok to Fremantle.

The pub keeps normal licensing hours on weekdays but closes on Sunday. They sell real-ale and the usual pub lunches.

SHEPHERD'S TAVERN
50 Hertford Street, W1

How to get there
The nearest Underground station is Green Park (Piccadilly Line). Turn right out of the station and walk west on Piccadilly to White Horse Street where you turn right and walk through to Hertford Street.

Shepherd's Tavern is a pub for the 'with it' crowd; the bright young people who choose to make it their local. They may live somewhere in the neighbourhood in a mews flat which once housed the Coachman who slept over the stable, and which has now become an expensive flat with a 'good' address.

As if to exemplify this process, the sedan chair of a long gone Duke of Cumberland has a prominent place in the bar and has now been converted to a telephone box.

Shepherd's Tavern is now the focal point of Shepherd's Market – a bright lively place in fashionable Mayfair, which somehow, in spite of being in the heart of London, retains the spirit of a village. Built by Edward Shepherd in 1735, it has a tiny square, a piazza and the tavern. It remains as Shepherd built it except that the plebeian shops are now boutiques or cute little restaurants. Nevertheless, it remains a small village surrounded by some of the most expensive residential property in London.

In the 50s it fell from grace when the 'pro's' haunted it, swinging their hips and giving lone tourists that 'Come on' look. Occasionally, the Police swept them up to appear before the Beak at Great Marlborough Street where they were fined a nominal sum. The girls became so familiar with the procedure that they would address the magistrate by his name – even enquiring after his health. But an Act of Parliament changed all this and the girls had to go underground.

Shepherd's attained it's finest hour during the Second World War when it became a rendezvous for the RAF. A member of an aircrew alone in town could always find congenial company in Shepherd's. Those of the RAF who were regulars could have their pewter mugs hung up behind the bar ready for their use when, or if, they came back. It was a lively place to be during the Battle of Britain when the pub kept a score board of the planes shot down on either side. It would be frequently adjusted while the customers cheered each German plane shot down.

Shepherd's has a good bow window to watch the bustle of life in the village. Naturally, they sell real ale and there is a running buffet upstairs during licensing hours which are 11 am to 11pm throughout the week.

RUNNING FOOTMAN
Charles Street, W1

How to get there
Underground (Piccadilly or Jubilee lines) to Green Park. Turn right out of station and walk west to Bolton Street. Walk along Bolton Street to Charles Street (second on left). Pub is on corner of Charles St and Hay Mews.

This Mayfair pub has an unusual name which hides a story. When the Grosvenors (who became the Dukes of Westminster) married into the Audleys, the family acquired land which stretched from Oxford Street down to the Thames. Successful land developers, they became fabulously rich by drawing rents from the lease of land to build houses on.

One of the people who built was the Duke of Queensbury whose family had a tradition of sporting interests (The Marquis of Queensbury laid down the rules of boxing) and the Duke maintained an athletic footman to run before his carriage in competition with other carriage owners who had men dressed in their own livery. The Queensbury's man could run at 7mph for many miles He carried a staff which concealed a concoction made from the white of eggs mixed with wine to refresh himself occasionally. His master was so proud of himself for establishing his running footman that he had a sign made up proclaiming 'I am the only running footman' which he exhibited at the pub which in turn claimed itself as having the longest sign of any pub in London. The sporting duke was prepared to back his man against any and many heroic contests took place starting from the pub.

Today the customers of the Running Footman may include a footman from one of the embassies or big houses in the neighbourhood – but you are more likely to meet bright young people who live in mews flats converted from the big houses, or maybe, a croupier from one of the gambling clubs.

The present day pub has the solid comfort of the Victorian era with the usual mahogany panelling and acid etched mirrors of the period. It isn't a particularly convivial pub – there is no music or any other form of distraction. The clientele are well dressed as befits the area; in short it is a pub of good solid comfort, well furnished, providing first class food. It conveys a sense of well-being.

PRINCESS LOUISE
High Holborn, WC1

How to get there
Underground to Holborn (Piccadilly or Central lines). From station going west, cross the main road into High Holborn. The pub is on the left close to Holborn Town Hall.

If you are looking for a warm, well lighted place with excellent food and good company, the Princess Louise will fill the bill. It is a great glistening pub with a single bar embracing the total floor space. The bar has a fine moulded ceiling and artistically engraved mirrors which reflect the warm lighting and rich panelling and bar fittings. It has the vibrant atmosphere that singles out the interesting pub.

A classic of its kind, it was named by the *Architects Journal* as being one of the six best pubs in London. It is located in a part of London which is difficult to classify, being on the fringe of Bloomsbury which is intellectual, yet close to St Giles which is not. The world centre of The Prudential Insurance is not too far away while the LCC School of Art and Lincoln's Inn (an abode of lawyers) is a stone's throw away. The quota of lawyers among it's customers might have been instrumental in persuading the London County Council to ban Developers from tearing down the fine old Georgian building in order to replace it with one of their cement and glass cubes that are so great for maximising rents.

The cuisine at the Princess Louise is outstanding. It draws a variegated crowd including many types and professions – they make interesting company.

TOURIST RETREATS

There comes a time in the Tourist's day when, sated with sights, fascinating as they may be, he or she would rather sit down to rest their feet while taking in sustenance.

The BTA (British Tourist Authority) are understanding about this weakness and have established restaurants and coffee shops under the roofs of such places as the National Art Gallery, the Tate Gallery and the British Museum, where, understanding that there may be a high proportion of foreigners amongst the clientele, they have tried to provide not only suitable surroundings but also appropriate food and drink.

Pubs, having survived for centuries by giving the public what it wants, have also got in on the act and you may be sure that wherever tourists swarm, there will be a pub handy.

THE TIGER
1 Tower Hill EC3.

How to get there
The nearest Underground station is Tower Hill (District and Circle lines). From the station follow pedestrian directions to The Tower of London. The Tiger is right by the entrance to the Tower, on historic Tower Hill.

The Tiger is the place to sit back and rest your feet after all those cobbled streets inside the Tower of London. There is a restaurant too. Inside the pub the various bars have names like Beefeater and Watchtower and are furnished appropriately.

Per square foot, the area outside the Tiger has witnessed more dark deeds than any other place in the Realm. Here Watt Tyler's men dragged Sir Robert Hales and Archbishop Sudbury from the Tower and hacked off their heads – ineptly as well as hideously. Here, in 1645, the Archbishop of Canterbury and three others were beheaded and their heads exhibited to the crowd. While the King, or officialdom, did their foul deeds inside the Tower, the Hoi Polloi did it's dirty work outside.

Unlike Tyburn, common criminals were not hanged here, rather it was a place for political vengeance to be exacted for the edification of the public. It still remains a venue for public outcry where orators stand, precariously, on a balustrade to exhort the crowd.

The pub puts out a story that the cat from the Tiger used to creep into the Tower to comfort Princess Elizabeth when she was a prisoner there.

William Penn was born in the vicinity. He was imprisoned for exhorting his political views in public. Later he left for America to found a home where Quakers could practice their style of life openly. It developed into The Commonwealth of Pennsylvania.

HOG IN THE POUND
South Molton Street, W1

How to get there
Nearest Underground station is Bond Street (Central and Jubilee lines). Turn right out of station and the pub will be in view on the triangle made by the intersection of South Molton and Davies streets.

This pub has the most lurid history. A former landlady, Catherine Hayes, was the last person in England to be burned alive as a punishment for murder. Her *modus operandi* was poisoning, which was committed on the premises. This might appear, on first glance, to reflect rather badly on the cuisine of the establishment ... but calm your fears, it happened 260 years ago. In fact, the cuisine in the present day Dive Bar is the reason why it attracts not only the locals but the shoppers from Oxford Street. It is just far enough back from the hurly-burly of the shopping thoroughfare to form a pleasant watering hole. Claridges Hotel, whose list of guests at any time resembles the Almanac de Gotha – updated to include oil billionaires, is a neighbour. It would be nice to say that it was their 'local' – but one is more likely to find a 'gentleman's gentleman' quaffing a pint there rather than an oil prince – although there might be a brace of croupiers from one of the gambling clubs relaxing after a late night shift.

The American Embassy is just up the street in Grosvenor Square, and in the summer one can usually find a covey of Americans sampling a real English pub.

The very unusual name of the pub comes by chance: the building was once the premises of a butcher who had a sign which showed an enormous hog enclosed in a pound. When he sold the premises he left the sign behind which was promptly put into service as a sign for the pub which it was to become.

JAZZ PUBS

A clarinet player once explained the mystique of playing jazz by saying 'You just kind of feel your way as you go.' which sums up the situation of jazz in pubs. They play for money of course, but also for the way they feel – playing a night here and a night there – only a handful of pubs can afford a regular band – mainly at weekends playing on Saturday night and at the Sunday lunchtime session. Some like The King's Head group, play when the theatre show is not on.

The pubs with the best atmosphere are those where a small combo plays in the bar ; feeling their way; responding artistically to the emotional support of their audience and in the process getting the place rocking.

The bar of a pub – not too small but definitely not too big – is ideally suited to the antecedents of jazz which started in the bordellos of New Orleans before a polite society recognised it.

When a gig gets under way in a crowded bar, the floor sways – even the ceiling threatens to join in. Nobody wants to go home when ''Time! Gentlemen please!'' sounds.

THE PRINCE OF ORANGE
118 Lower Road, Rotherhithe, SE16

How to get there
Underground to Surrey Docks station (East London line from Whitechapel. To Whitechapel by District Line). Turn left out of the station on to Lower Road. Walk north on Lower Road to Prince of Orange (10 minutes).

The pub is a jazz freak's dream. In an atmosphere as near as you may get to the New Orleans honky tonks where jazz began, players join with their fans to relish the music.

The players – trumpet, trombone, clarinet, piano – improvise as they go since there is no score and no particular leader. Maybe a chord from the piano will suggest a theme to slide into, maybe a request shouted from the bar.

The fans who are as much a part of the show as the players, strut, weave, shake and snap fingers and jerk spasmodically in time to the beat. A girl writhes her lissome young body to express her emotions in body language. Each one is sealed in a personal world, yet they are part of the whole, conjoined in a mystic ceremony.

Jazz has come a long way from New Orleans or the Chicago 'Speak Easy'. It has even been taken up by the intellectuals – not that the Cockneys of Rotherhithe sit sedately in the Orchestra Stalls or at a table served by waiters. They want to be 'Wiv it!' They want to be close enough to the instruments to feel their vibrations going through them. On jazz nights they crowd so close to the players that a trombone may slide over their heads. The bar becomes so crowded that once trapped on a settee between wall and table, one requires some Houdini like manoeuvres to get up to the bar. But, some kindly soul will hand your drink and change over to you because the music joins everybody into the same happy party.

When the Potman begins to shout "Time Gentlemen Please!" to get you out, he is ignored. By law, closing time is 11pm but at 11.30 they are still in earnest discussion about Louis Armstrong or Fats Waller.

"Ain't you got no bleedin' 'ome?" the Potman bleats.

The Pianist slings his jacket over his shoulder and pushes his way to the door, but is soon abducted to settle a musical argument.

The trumpet player is inveigled and snatches of Tiger Rag come from that direction.

The Landlord orders the door to be propped open and cool, damp air seeps in from the river.

A girl in a flimsy dress shivers but accepts a young man's jacket and stays. Nobody wants to break up the party, but finally one comes out into the streets of Rotherhithe – east of Tower Bridge. A place where your bowler hatted, umbrella carrying West Ender would not be seen even with an unrolled umbrella. But it contains some interesting pubs.

THE NEW MERLIN'S CAVE
Margery Street, WC1

How to get there
Underground to Farrington Station (Metropolitan line) from station walk north on Farringdon Road over Rosebury Avenue to King's Cross Road. Margery Street is on right.

There really is a cave; bats cannot be guaranteed and there is no resident magician unless you count the leader of the jazz band that plays there, but the moulded arch of the cave's roof is lit with an eerie light that creates a nocturnal mood.

The indented surface of the roof tend to soak up the sound rather than make it reverberate around the cave but the audience give the usual support – 'Yeh! yeh!-ing', tapping glasses and feet. The Sunday session, in spite of the short hours (12.00 to 2.00pm) is the event of the week. From Wednesday to Saturdays, the sessions run beyond midnight.

Merlin was a Welsh Wizard which is the motif patterned into the carpet in the foyer. It indicates the care taken to create the illusion of sorcery. A bar in the cave has been fitted and melds in with its surrounding as to suggest it just grew there. That which embellishes the mood is provided in the shape of a variety of Real Ales on draught in this Free House. Hot and cold food is available.

The customers are not of any specific calling and are of all ages. The only thing they have in common is the love of jazz – maybe the unique atmosphere contributes, too. Jazz fans are liable to give spontaneous expression to their mood, here there is plenty of room to indulge in any form of expression including dancing in the shadows of the cave.

REAL ALE

Most of the problems of packaging food and drink are connected with keeping the product fresh until it is ready for consumption. This problem is too often solved to the detriment of its taste.

When a barrel of beer leaves the brewery it continues to mature in the barrel. It requires great care on the part of the pub's landlord to prevent the beer "going off" while it is waiting to be consumed. Good pubs are referred to as 'having good cellars' (ie; the landlord knows how to keep his cellar in good condition). To obviate this problem, breweries took to the practice of pasteurising the beer before it left the brewery. The beer was pumped into metal kegs and put under the pressure of carbon dioxide which 'killed' the beer but rendered it unnaturally fizzy and altered the flavour. This beer saved the pub landlord a great deal of trouble in maintaining his cellar at proper temperature and at switching barrels judiciously.

More and more of the breweries began to introduce the keg beer into the pubs they owned, until a band of stalwart beer drinkers determined to protect their favourite tipple took action by forming CAMRA (Campaign for Real Ale) and looked round for breweries that still produced real-ale.

It is a fact of life that the further north one goes from the south coast of England, the better the beer becomes. The ales of many a Northern and Midlands brewery – with the support of CAMRA - began to appear in London's pubs. Names like Marston, Samuel Smith, Ruddle, Webster, appeared. Bruce's brewery even made their beer on the premises of their pubs to ensure that it was fresh.

Your common or garden beer drinker swallowed the idea – copiously – with the result that, nowadays, real ales are available in most London pubs. Real-ale pubs take pride in stocking as many different ales as their cellars will hold. As for the real-ale drinkers... their aim is to sample the lot.

SUN INN

63 Lambs Conduit Street, WC1

How to get there

Nearest Underground station Russell Square (Piccadilly line). Turn left out of station to Russell Hotel. Turn left into Southampton Row and continue south to Guildford Street. Turn left into Guildford Street and walk down to Lambs Conduit Street on right. Sun is on right hand side of street.

The atmosphere of the Sun is male and hearty. Most of the drinking is done standing up which, a real ale drinker will tell you, calls on the power of gravity to assist in the pleasurable task of consumption. There is no question of eavesdropping in this establishment since conversation is carried out at about half gale level on the Beauford scale in many accents including foreign – particularly in the tourist season because the area is stuffed with hotels both great and small.

People are extremely friendly here; the fact that you are there at all, implies that you are a serious beer drinker and therefore have much in common with the other acolytes.

The list of ales exhibited on the wall behind the bar resembles the departure board at King's Cross station in its fecundity since they claim to stock the draught ales of 70 different breweries in the cellars below deck, they include guest ales from places like Rutland which has, since our visit, disappeared.

This is a great place for the loner to visit since he may simply turn to the person next to him and join in conversation.

WEST END

The part of London which Londoners call 'The West End' is not situated in the west end of London but occupies roughly a square mile in the centre of the city. It is the part which includes most of the good restaurants and big stores the Royal Palace and the art galleries, it is the pleasure ground of London. Pubs in The West End vary from the Dog and Dock which has a tiny bar on either side of the service counter, to the Chandos at Trafalgar Square, which is tramped by thousands every day; amongst them are pubs which because they are frequented by sophisticated types who like to meet sophisticated people, may fairly be described as West End pubs.

THE SALISBURY
St Martin's Lane, WC1

How to get there
Take the Underground (Northern line) to Leicester Square. From the station walk 1 minute south on Charing Cross Road to St Martin's Court. Walk down the narrow court to St Martin's Lane. The pub is on the corner of St Martin's Lane and the court.

The atmosphere of the Salisbury – carefully preserved over the years – is that of the Victorian era. There are settees upholstered in red plush confronted by marble topped tables, the walls are adorned by beautiful etched and bevelled mirrors, aspidistras in Clisonne pots, lamp brackets that look like gas brackets and in the main bar of three, a massive mahogany bar counter. A large inner parlour they call the lounge is decorated with murals painted all round the walls. A tiny bar called the Snug which is entered from St Martin's Court conveys a sense of intimacy not present in the main Saloon bar from which the pub takes its personality. The people lounging on the settees are well dressed with here and there a touch of individuality; they give the bar an air of sophistication. From the front door on St Martin's Lane, one can see four theatres and it comes as no surprise to find that the Salisbury is an actor's pub; that is, frequented by actors, the pub does not present a show, in fact the only form of entertainment offered is conversation or watching the actors giving imitations of a mean landlady in Scunthorpe or a railway porter in Dublin- "Sure" 'tis only actors and fish that travel on a Sunday!;".

If you like to observe Homo Sapiens the Salisbury is your bag. At one time it was invaded by the so called Gays. It was amusing to watch because they were the flamboyant type. This is probably a temporary phase. In any case the Salisbury is too widely known by too many people with divergent interests to allow of it becoming a Gay pub. The Lounge used to be presided over by a little French waiter called Albert who always wore tails and a stiff shirt. With Gallic flair, Albert rendered a performance of how a "san-viche" and a bottle of wine should be served that could not be improved on by any of the actors present. The food is the usual Pub food, but sandwiches can be made to order. It is the people rather than the food which is the main attraction of the Salisbury.

NEWBORN PUBS

Since London became the tourist capital of the world, the authorities have been busy pulling down and rebuilding it – in some cases to its advantage. All the decrepit buildings along the Thames embankment between Waterloo and London Bridge on the south bank have been cleared so that visitors may walk the route.

Before the clearing of what were merely industrial buildings places such as the site of the Globe theatre of Shakespeare's day, Cardinal Wolsey's house and The Bear Garden had, over the centuries, virtually disappeared being hemmed in by slums. Now excavations are in hand to uncover sites of The Globe and The Rose, theatres. A museum has been established on the site.

This was the pleasure ground of London in the 16th century, inevitably there would have been pubs.

Pubs, rarely disappear; they get rebuilt over the centuries and sometimes change their names – the Mayflower which is associ- ated with the ship of that name, was once call The Shippe. The Tabard from where Geoffrey Chaucer and his pilgrims set out on their pilgrimage to Canterbury may now be a non descript pub in a dreary area nowadays, but it is a descendant of the original Inn.

Usually as a result of large rebuilding schemes, new pubs get built. Covent Garden Market is relocated from its previous site to a new site at Nine Elms; manifestly, at least one new pub is a necessity for whoever knew a market porter who didn't need his pint for breakfast? The clearing of sites along the river; the redundancy of places like St Catherine's Dock, make the building of new pubs desirable, hence The Dickens is built. Pubs like the Founders Arms appear, on Bankside. The Punch & Judy in the new Covent Garden which is no longer a market but a tourists resort, is build to provide the tourists with a view of an English pub. They start without a history which is a handicap, for, pubs form the historic background as much as kings and cause a lot less trouble.

THE DICKENS
St. Katherine's Dock, Tower Hill

How to get there
Underground, Tower Hill (District or Circle line). From station follow signs to S$^{t.}$ Katherine's Dock. Enter through the dock gate and follow the basins round to the Dickens in a nautical environment of the 18th century.

The pub is by no means a local, but in the evening it is popular with Londoners, because the English have a 'thing' for the sea. Saint Katherine's dock was once crowded with tall ships bringing cargoes of tea from China or wool from Australia. Humbler ships brought wine from Bordeaux or mahogany from Honduras, but the dock could not take large ships and, although the nearest dock to the City of London, it fell into neglect. Now it has been given a 'spit and polish' and been restored to use for pleasure as a yacht marina. The pub, called The Dickens after you-know-who, is in a corner of the dock farthest removed from the main gate, and one traverses cobble-stoned walks past the various basins sheltering a motley collection of sloops, ketches, yawls and the old Nore lightship. Although tricked out in a shining scarlet paint, the old professional from the Nore looks slightly forlorn amongst all these amateurs. It is berthed right outside The Dickens. It brings up personal memories of a bewildered sailor − trying to fix his bearings amidst myriad lights winking and flashing around the horizon − that here was one fix that could be relied upon. Now it peers through the mullioned windows of the pub at a collection of wines, spirits and real-ales as long as a yardarm. The wines and spirits are all drawn from separate casks painted with names like 'Madeira' or 'Barbados' or 'Bordeaux'. Bearing in mind the reputation of 'Jolly Jack' no pub would be allowed within the precincts of the old dock and it is a safe bet that The Dickens is of recent vintage. The food is modern and excellent with a leaning towards English food. The illusion of sailing ship days is not carried to the point of serving hard tack or salted beef.

The surroundings to the dock are the genuine article; across the way the turrets of the Tower of London, looking curiously diminished by the new high-rise buildings behind it, give no inkling of the horrors were perpetrated in it's dungeons. But the neighbouring Royal Mint looks sturdy enough to bar the way to the gold held in it's cellars.

Yes! the oak ceiling beams, the rough deal tables the low ceilings, do foster the illusion of being aboard a sailing ship. A visit to The Dickens set in it's appropriately nautical atmosphere is a nostalgic trip back to the days when Britannia ruled the waves.

CHELSEA

Chelsea is a district that lives on its reputation as an "Arty" place where painters and writers live a Bohemian existence. It is true that Thomas Carlyle, Henry Fielding, John Gay, Whistler and Rossetti all lived there at one time or another. The Chelsea Arts Ball – a razamatazz held every year by students, also gave it a Bohemian association, but it could now be more accurately described as a place where stockbrokers live in workmens cottages expensively converted into pieds-a-terre. The King's Road which is the spine of Chelsea is for the young of all nations who are attracted to the latest outrage in fashions sold in the shops that line the King's Road.

ADMIRAL CODRINGTON
17 Mossop Street, Chelsea, SW3

How to get there
Underground to South Kensington. Walk down Pelham Street to Draycott Avenue then left into Mossop Street.

A lively pub full of Yuppies and Students who come here mainly to talk and not *soto voco* either, it has a half dozen ramshackle bars furnished in a Victorian style. On the walls framed accounts written in the elaborate copperplate of the period are accounts of the battles of the gallant admiral for whom the pub is named. As a captain commanding HMS Orion at Trafalgar he gave such a splendid account of himself that Lord Nelson promoted him to Admiral. The fact that his name is better known as a pub in Chelsea nowadays is an indication that admirals may come and go but pubs live on for ever. Judging by the way bars have been added, the pub has flourished over the years and its reputation has spread until what was a Local in a backstreet has become a well known place. What was once a conservatory at the back of the building has been pressed into service as a bar.

A long planted vine whose branches are now as thick as a man's wrist has twined its way up to the glass roof to look down on the customers – mainly students in this bar. A kid wearing a New York Yankee's baseball cap is declaiming to a circle of his pals his views on Art with all the authority of a twenty year old. There is a Chelsea Arts Ball held every year when the students go haywire. Another group with "Down Under" accents are drinking Foster's lager on draught at the bar at the end of the conservatory.

There is a wide variety of ales served in the other bars and of course the usual spirits and wines and there is a restaurant next door where the Chelsea spirit is apparent; tiny tables are positioned to fit into whatever space is available, by a six foot West Indian waitress with an engaging smile who manages to slither through to serve the excellent food. The menu is a mixture of English foods like rack of lamb with redcurrant sauce and International foods like poached salmon. With food like this available the pub does not bother with the usual pub snacks.

The Admiral Coodrigton is definitely an evening pub where it is not only the young who go to talk; plenty of mature people frequent it who tend to be well educated. Its atmosphere is typical of Chelsea which I would describe as; bright, lively, loquacious.

CHELSEA POTTER
119 Kings Road SW3

How to get there
Underground (District or Circle line) to Sloane Square. From station walk west along King's Road (3 minutes). The Chelsea Potter is on the left.

The Kings Road, which is the spine of Chelsea, is a meeting place for the young of all nations, who are attracted by the latest in fashions sold in the many clothes shops there.

The Chelsea Potter is average in the matter of food and drink, except for the fact that they sell Strongbow on draught. Strongbow is a cider. Do not confuse it with mere apple juice. It is virulently alcoholic.

The great point about the Chelsea Potter is its casual friendliness. Sitting outside, one can watch a youthful world go by. This is the place where you are likely to see the Apache haircuts and hair dyed purple or green and clothes designed to impress ... and to shock.

While sitting outside the Chelsea Potter, I watched a small drama of frustrated love. At the curb a girl sat in a car. The back wheels of the car had been locked by the police with a huge clamp that only they could release. She was drinking pints of Strongbow, obviously trying to get drunk. As she finished one, she would get out of the car to fetch another, then go back.

A young Dutchman with a French girlfriend, who was sitting at the same bench as myself, explained in English, and then in French, what was happening. They had witnessed a blazing row between the girl and her German boyfriend, who had stalked off with the ignition key, leaving the car illegally parked. The boyfriend had to come back sometime. Meanwhile, the girl sat in the car drinking Strongbow. The young Dutchman and his girl sat waiting for the highlight – the return of the German. I just sat and waited too, not so much for the emotion of the *rencontre*, but to satisfy my curiosity as to what form it would take. When it happened, the girl threw a pint of Strongbow in his face, then burst into tears and threw her arms around his neck in a loving embrace. The audience whistled and applauded. So much for a slice of life in the Kings Road.

SIX BELLS TAVERN
King's Road, Chelsea, SW3

How to get there
Underground (District & Circle lines) to Sloan Square, then by any of the buses 11,19,22,49, going west on King's Road. Get off at the Old Town Hall.

If you are in the market for an oil painting, try the Six Bells. Chelsea artists exhibit their paintings here. Whistler and Rossetti both knew its pleasant garden and would sit under the mulberry tree on fine summer days. Maybe to trundle a few 'woods' down its bowling green. The house they knew has been rebuilt but the fountain still arcs its crystal spray in the air.

The thoroughfare from Sloane Square towards Stamford Bridge was once the private road of the King (Charles II) when he travelled to visit his favourite mistress Nell Gwynn. It was Nell who persuaded him to build the Royal Hospital for old sailors and soldiers in Chelsea. The long scarlet coats of the Chelsea pen- sioners are a familiar sight in the Six Bells. Any of them will gracefully accept a drink and relate the history of the Hospital or tell stories of past wars.

Chelsea is famous for its boutiques. To watch the girls bouncing along the King's road is to get an advance view of youthful fashion. It is also the home of the Chelsea Football club which has broken more hearts than Casanova. In the bar of the Six Bells you can distinguish a Chelsea football fan by his habit of prefixing the name Chelsea by an expletive.

The Six Bells is a large pub which also houses a disco at weekends. It has pub food but also a restaurant. It has the normal opening hours.

KNIGHTSBRIDGE

Knightsbridge is not only a thoroughfare containing the exclusive premises of the Royal Yacht Squadron, but at its tradesman's entrance, the likes of Harrods. It is not so much a place for the filthy rich as the exquisitely rich.

PAXTON'S HEAD
Knightsbridge, SW3

How to get there
Underground to Knightsbridge station, walk west on Knightsbridge to where it forks at Brompton Road. Paxton's Head is opposite the Horse Guards barracks in Knights-bridge.

This tastefully furnished example of a Victorian pub is a local for the people who live in the mansions adjacent and for the troopers of the Royal Horse Guards who live opposite. Although quite friendly the two groups do not mix. The civilians sit quietly conversing in the accents of the more expensive Public Schools while the, noisier, soldiers call between each other in a scatter of accents. The theory involved in knocking down the partitions that previously segregated the customers was to introduce a spirit of democracy, but it made no difference people still prefer to be with their own kind.

Bereft of their martial uniforms and sphinx like stare, the trooper appears like any other young man when wearing a sports shirt and slacks; except for the odd, "Insider" jokes about their duties while escorting royalty, but the jokes were invariably on themselves – not the Royals. They had obviously been trained not to talk about any member of the Royal household.

The pub is named after the man who built the Crystal Palace. Paxton was a Go Getter who perfected the art of constructing large buildings of glass and steel. Originally a gardener on the staff of the Duke of Devonshire, he became a Member of Parliament and was knighted.

The Paxton is a very civilised pub, it gives the impression that nothing so uncivilised as a brawl or even an ugly word could be uttered there. Sometimes a ''Gentleman's Gentleman will drop in to take a glass of Madeira and peruse the evening paper in a calm and dignified way. It is a good pub to sit and observe others.

INDEX